RENEWING YOUR MIND

RENEWING YOUR MIND

THINKING AS A CHRISTIAN

• • • • • • • • • • • • • •

A 11-SESSION SMALL GROUP EXPLORATION
VIA DIALOG OF A CHRISTIAN WORLDVIEW

WRITTEN BY
JACK DANNEMILLER

ADAPTED FOR USE BY SMALL GROUPS BY
BRIAN REGRUT

DEDICATION

To my beloved Jean Marie who is home in Heaven now with her Lord Jesus Christ and to our two sons David and Peter their wives Suzanne and Ginger and to our four grandchildren, Jack, Halley, Kate and Caroline.

Renewing Your Mind
© 2021 Living Dialog Ministries
PO Box 15125
Richmond, VA 23227

All Rights Reserved

Published in the United States of America by Living Dialog Ministries, a 501(c)(3) tax exempt organization. www.livingdialog.org

ISBN 978-0-9890791-6-7

Scripture quotations, unless otherwise indicated, are taken from the HOLY BIBLE NEW INTERNATIONAL VERSION. Copyright © 1973, 1978, 1984, 2011 by International Bible Society. Used by permission of Zondervan. All rights reserved.

Cover and interior design by Frank Gutbrod

18 17 16 15 14 13 7 6 5 4 3 2 1

Printed in the United States of America

CONTENTS

FOREWORD by Allen Hye, Phd *01*

PREFACE *04*

INTRODUCTION *07*

SESSION 1: A Journey of Discovery: What does it mean to Think as a Christian? *13*

SESSION 2: How does studying history help one formulate a worldview? *17*

SESSION 3: What role should theology play in developing a worldview? *23*

SESSION 4: How should a Christian view the Nature of Man? *33*

SESSION 5: How does understanding the Origins of Man help you relate to God? *39*

SESSION 6: In what way does Natural and Biblical Law provide a foundation for a Christian worldview *49*

SESSION 7: How should a Biblical understanding of marriage and family guide a Christian's worldview? *55*

SESSION 8: How do government and politics influence the life of a Christian? *65*

SESSION 9: How does a Biblical worldview help you evaluate competing economic systems? *73*

SESSION 10: How does a Christian view of social justice mesh with a secular view? *83*

SESSION 11: How does your worldview align with Biblical principles? *90*

EPILOGUE *96*

APPENDIX *98*

ACKNOWLEDGEMENTS *115*

FOREWORD

Summit Ministries defines a worldview as "any ideology, philosophy, theology, movement or religion that provides an overarching approach to understanding God, the world, and the relationship of people to God and the world." We all have a worldview, even if unconsciously and without formally articulating it. It is our take on the nature of the world, like a lens through which we view and try to comprehend life. If the lens is faulty, if the prescription is wrong, our view of the world will be faulty and blurry. Such an uninformed and out-of-focus view will lead to poor decisions, bad behavior, and an unfulfilling life. We need a focused view, formed by a perfect lens.

The prophet Hosea warns, "My people are destroyed for lack of knowledge" (Hosea 4:6). It is incumbent on us all to pursue knowledge about the world, God's creation, in order to cultivate a worldview that is true to reality. Developing a Christian, or Biblical, worldview requires seeing the real world through the divine lens of God's Word, the Holy Bible.

This book by my good friend Jack Dannemiller, a veteran Bible teacher and small group discussion leader, will help you and your study group do just that. If the idea of developing a Biblical worldview at first sounds daunting, it need not be so. Jack and his collaborators have published several successful small group studies. They will be your tour guides as they lead you on a journey through nine prominent fields of human endeavor and inquiry. Here is what this journey to a biblical worldview will include:

- *A call to* renew our minds, so that we might be transformed by the light of God's Word;
- An understanding of the basics, the core of each discipline in this study;
- The foundational beliefs of the Christian faith, whether you are learning them for the first time or reviewing them to strengthen your Christian walk;
- The reliability of the Bible, your guide to living and the foundation of our Christian worldview;
- A search for truth–not ideology or bias–as you investigate each discipline on the journey;
- An awareness of hot-button issues in today's culture, such as evolution, social justice, marriage and family, the capitalism vs. socialism debate, and the proper function of government.

The layout of this book will further facilitate your group study by presenting chapters of manageable length, each interspersed with helpful discussion questions that will train you to think like a Christian as you progress through the material. The final chapter consists of a summary of each chapter, snapshots of the exciting stops along your journey, which allow for review of the entire study.

I am pleased to commend this book to your group study and pray that you all may, through the leading of the Holy Spirit, renew your minds by developing a Biblical worldview and thinking like a Christian.

Allen E. Hye, Ph.D.

Dr. Hye, Professor Emeritus at Wright State University, is author of *The Moral Dilemma of the Scientist in Modern Drama* and *The Great God Baseball: Religion in Modern Baseball Fiction*. He has also served as strategic educational consultant with College For Less, Inc. and taught adult Christian education courses on Great Hymns of the Christian Faith. Allen and his wife of 50+ years, Roberta, are residents of Fort Myers, Florida and attend Sanibel Community Church.

PREFACE

In our culture hardly a day goes by when there is a reference to your mind. Some references are humorous. Some others serious and some are sad. Here are some of the frequent statements we all hear routinely;

- Have you lost your mind?
- Are you out of your mind?
- My mind used to be like a steel trap.
- Mind your manners!
- Do you mind the cold weather?
- Mind your own business!
- What's on your mind?
- Don't fill your mind with 'garbage'!

This is but a small sample of thoughts from every day references to your mind. So, if the mind is often, 'Top of Mind', then our minds must be and important part of our human nature. That being said, these questions come to mind, no pun intended:

- Where is your mind?
- What is its purpose?
- Is it possible to renew your mind?

- Is there a process to renew your mind?
- What is a transformed mind?
- What is the relationship between your mind and your conscience?
- Is it possible have a peace of mind with God?
- Is it possible for you have a mind filled with wisdom like King Solomon?

There are so many questions in life. That's what makes life and its journey exciting; discovering answers to some of the profound questions in life such as, Is it possible to transform your mind? What would a transformed mind look like? Is it important to transform your mind?

Your mind and its ability to enable you to reason, think, understand, discern, discover and learn is what differentiates mankind from all other creatures. Your mind is an eternal component of your 'being'. It is an essential part of a person being, "Created in the Image of God".

In this book we will explore together the process for transforming and renewing your mind so that overtime you could have, 'The Mind of Christ'. That doesn't mean you will be omniscient like Him but you will be able to see and understand the world around you and the culture we live in from God's perspective.

The fascinating truth is that on this journey you will acquire a Biblical worldview that is, our world as God sees it. Such a worldview will guide your decision-making, establish your core values and shape your life to honor God and Jesus Christ in all you do. It will also allow you to enjoy being in the presence of God now, and for all eternity.

Along this journey you will find that Peace with God which is beyond our human understanding. You will be enabled to become an ambassador for Christ wherever you go in life. You will become a partner with Him in building God's kingdom. So, enjoy the journey. Blessings await!

INTRODUCTION

In his textbook, *Thinking like a Christian*, David Noebel States that everyone has a worldview but has a tough time articulating clearly what they hold true. In a dialogue on societal issues, cultural trends, economics, politics, philosophy, origins of man or theological considerations just saying that you believe something to be true, even if it is, seldom strikes a chord of agreement with the others involved. Christians, atheists and even agnostics and those of other religions all have a set of beliefs or core values that define how they view life and make choices.

Core values are those set of standards or filters to which they process various inputs and make important life decisions. In fact, when people are asked about their values and beliefs most answers would be surprisingly similar. Many would respond with words like integrity, honesty, truth, openness, compassion, et cetera. These are certainly desirable values although different cultures and different religions will define them uniquely to fit their purposes. In America today even truth seems to be relative, that is, my truth vs. your truth; even God's truth as described in the Bible, and scientific and mathematical truth are debated ad nauseam. Logically there can only be one truth. However, values like integrity or morality vary greatly by culture and religion.

How a nation defines its culture and its aspirations are key elements of its worldview. A shared worldview enables a nation's people to experience a unity of purpose and a spirit of patriotism. For example, America was founded on Judeo-Christian principles and values established by God in the Bible. The Constitution and the Declaration of Independence reflect those values. America is a nation of laws guided by the 10 commandments and the teachings of Jesus. It's the willingness of people to follow these laws that makes for a safe and just society. American Christians understand that one day they will stand before God to give an accounting of their lives. They are reminded of that whenever they recite "One nation under God", or read "In God We Trust" on our coins and currency.

In his book, *To Know With Certainty*, Lee Southard lays out the facts and evidence for the impact that Christianity has had on shaping Western civilization and the truth needed to both proactively contend for and defend the Christian faith. In effect, Southard's book sets forth much of the foundational information to be able to think like a Christian.

This 11 week study takes a look at just nine of the essential topics that impact a worldview. It also addresses the idea from the Great Commandment which Jesus affirmed in Matthew 22:37 you shall "Love the Lord your God with all your heart and with all your soul and with all your mind." Jesus then expanded that commandment to include loving your neighbor as yourself. Christianity must be a faith of both the heart, and the mind. Love and compassion must be buttressed by reason and rationality. Christians must be equipped to engage in the dialog about worldview so that they are able to shine the light of Christ's love and Biblical truth into an ever more darkening Post-Christian world.

Each session provides questions for discussion making the role of the Group leader easier to facilitate. No advance preparation is required. This study is an invitation for the participants to engage in dialog which is the method Jesus often used; asking and answering profound questions. In dialog the goal is to inquire, explore and discover and to seek understanding. We will be looking for Biblical truths which define the worldview on each of the chapter topics. The first chapter is extremely important as it sets the stage for what follows with the question; What does it mean to Think as a Christian? So fasten your seatbelt, put on your thinking cap, open your mind and heart and enjoy this fast paced journey of discovering your worldview and learning to think as a Christian with a renewed mind.

Kinds of dialogs

There are different kinds of dialogs we will experience during our gatherings:

- *Dialog with God* — We believe that God calls each of us to a relationship with him. This relationship gives meaning and purpose to our lives. God wants deep, personal, and open communication with us.

- *Dialog with self* — As you think about what Thinking as a Christian means for the church in the 21st century, you may have thoughts and feelings that clarify, stretch, and challenge your understanding of Jesus and Christianity. You may think, "Is that what Jesus really meant?", "I wonder what the Bible is really saying by that?" or "I never thought about it that way before."

- *Dialog with others who are physically present* — The exchange of thoughts and feelings amplify and deepen your understanding. Some of us learn of Jesus, the Bible and Christianity from the word of others. Listening is a powerful tool for discovery.

- *Dialog with others who aren't present* — The words and ideas of others you've known interact with your own thoughts and shape your perceptions in both positive and negative ways.

Invitation to dialog

The kind of dialog we want to cultivate in our group is not another word for "discussion" or "debate". Discussion is analytical and typically picks things apart. In debate, sides work to win points. Dialog, on the other hand, is a way for us together to seek understanding.

Dialog is intended:
- not to advocate but inquire
- not to argue but explore
- not to convince but discover

We listen to one another to find out what is meant. We assume each member of the group has a piece of the answer to the question, and that together, the group can craft a new and better answer. We celebrate new insights, greater clarity, and deeper understandings when they occur.

Agreement is not the purpose of dialog. It is important to suspend judgment about others' contributions. Disagreements can be seen as a different way of looking at a subject. Disagreements can energize a group to seek meaning and clarity that goes beyond initial conflicting views.

How to use this guide

These 11 sessions will guide your group in dialog with one another through powerful messages about competing worldviews, underpinnings of American democracy and Biblical truth.

This guide couldn't be simpler to use. No advance preparation or study is required! Some groups may choose to begin each gathering with prayer, or take a few minutes to catch up on one another's lives.

To launch into your time of dialog, your facilitator or someone from your group will read a few brief paragraphs. Immediately following each section, you'll find a question or two designed to launch your group into dialog over the ideas and issues raised in the text. Your group should stop at the end of each segment to consider the questions that are posed before moving onto the next segment of text. The questions will look like this:

> ■ Are you open to experiencing a spiritual transformation? Why or why not?

You'll find additional questions at the end of each session if your group is looking for further discussion or personal reflection.

Plan on an hour or so for dialog for each meeting. Some groups have gone far beyond an hour due to the intensity and enjoyment of the dialog. Your group's facilitator should be sensitive to the time commitment each member has made to the group. Make sure those in the group agree to go beyond the stated time if extended discussion time seems to be warranted.

Remember that your group's facilitator is there not as an answer man or woman, but as a coach. Each member of your group brings insight and value to the dialog as you craft an answer together. Your facilitator will help to honor your group's time commitment and guide you through the material each week.

You'll close each session with dialog in prayer. Affirming that Christ has been with you as you've shared this Biblically focused group experience each week is the foundation for this time. Members of your group may have needs in their lives or questions and concerns raised through the session's dialog. This guide offers some general tips about how to pray conversationally, as well as suggestions for how to shape your prayer experience. Prayer may not be a familiar discipline to you—but it can be as simple as dialoging with a friend. And you are!

Each person must make his or her own decision whether to become a follower of Jesus or not. This decision has eternal implications. We hope and pray that you and your group enjoy your journey of discovery. May each member be blessed, challenged, and encouraged as you develop a greater understanding of a Christian worldview. Ok, let's get started.

SESSION 1

A JOURNEY OF DISCOVERY: WHAT DOES IT MEAN TO THINK AS A CHRISTIAN?

A Christian or Biblical worldview requires looking at the disciplines that make up the culture of American society. The Christian belief system, which is grounded in both fact and divine revelation is relevant to all of life. This journey will investigate whether a Christian worldview is the only one based on truth, God's truth.

Alexis De Tocqueville, the French politician and philosopher who toured America in the 1830's and penned the most comprehensive report of the young country, wrote: "there is no country in the world, in which the Christian religion retains a greater influence over all the souls of men than in America." If Tocqueville were to report on America today his assessment would undoubtedly be different. Not only has politics, commerce and society changed in the past 190 years, so too has Christianity.

- What is the evidence that Christianity's influence on American culture has changed?
- If this influence has been diminished, what can individuals do to recover it?
- What should the church's role be in recovering this influence?

Are Christians in America experiencing the 'boiled frog syndrome'? In other words, have they failed to see the gradual deterioration in moral values, the decline in Church attendance and the loss of its youth to the secular culture? Are they not concerned enough about the multi-billion dollar abortion industry, the rise in addiction to drugs and pornography, the violent video games and immoral movies, and issues like gender identity, Critical Race Theory, gay marriage, the 1619 project and the breakdown of family life?

- Which of the above strikes you as being most harmful to the American society?
- What actions should be taken to counter this harmful influence?

The family is one of the most important and foundational institutions for maintaining a stable and free society. We will look at this in depth in Session 7 but we need to be thinking about the role of parents in passing along their wisdom and values.

> **Why has it become increasingly difficult for parents to communicate with their children?**

This study is a 'call to arms' to win the battle for the survival of Christian influence in America's society and culture. Human rights, religious freedoms, criminal justice, political freedoms, economic prosperity and the rule of law have flourished in cultures that have embraced a Christian and Biblical worldview. The battle is both intellectual and spiritual. There seems to be forces that are trying to destroy the credibility of the Bible and the Christian worldview. If Western Civilization, as we know it and enjoy it today, is dependent upon the continuation of a Christian worldview what will the future look like? Should society adhere to God's creative and redemptive orders for life as found in the Bible?

Faith is the central problem of this age, the post-Christian era. When nations and men forgot God, they experienced, in the 20th Century alone, the inhumanity, wickedness and moral depravity of Nazism, Socialism and Communism and the extinction of tens of millions of human lives. These and other 'isms' fall within the realm of the elemental forces of the world. They are based on the wisdom of this world and are a grand deception of Satan. Secular humanism, post modernism and cosmic humanism are precipitating a further decline in human morality and further separation from the goodness and love of God in the 21st-century. Albert Einstein, though not a Christian, observed that where God is absent evil will flourish. Blasé Pascal, a 16th century philosopher, was convinced there is a God-shaped vacuum in the human soul that only God's Holy Spirit can fill.

- How do 21st century Americans, try to fill the God-shaped vacuum in the human soul?
- Describe the satisfaction individuals derive from trying to fill this vacuum.

The Apostle Paul, who was the most influential follower of Jesus, said Christians must fearlessly proclaim the good news of the gospel including creation, Christ's life and resurrection, and pending judgment. (Ephesians 6:19) He understood that Christianity was not so much a religion as it was a worldview.

As we journey through this guide think about those core principles that will shape our thinking, renew our minds, give us understanding of the Christian worldview and allow us all to influence those around us for God's kingdom through Christ Jesus.

"As Christians we are tempted to make unnecessary concessions to those outside of faith. We give in too much...We must show our Christian colors if we are to be true to Christ—We can't remain silent or concede everything away."

C.S.Lewis

SESSION 2

HOW DOES STUDYING HISTORY HELP ONE FORMULATE A WORLDVIEW?

A Biblical worldview starts with history—His-Story. It is God's story that preexists the creation of the universe, continues through the final judgment of mankind, and extends into eternity.

The Bible is the key to world events past, present and future. Archaeology has consistently supported and verified the assertion that the Bible is a trustworthy historical document. The Bible is the best documented of all ancient historical books. The Bible claims to be the inspired Word of God. It has shown itself to be so by the hundreds of predictions exactly fulfilled years and centuries after they were made. This is so because God knows the entire experience of the human race as if it has already happened.

- How is the Bible the key to world events and a book of history?
- How can we trust the Bible as an accurate portrayal of His — Story?

The Bible was written by 40 authors over a period of 1500 years without contradiction as the content flows harmoniously from Genesis through Revelation. Historical events described in the Bible were primarily written by eyewitnesses to those events with the exception being events described in Genesis that were told to Moses directly by God. The Bible is the best selling book of all times because it contains God's truth and wisdom and is the operating manual for living a meaningful and purposeful life. Some have described it as Best Investigated Before Leaving Earth.

- How and when did Moses get the history written in Genesis?
- In what language is the original old testament Scripture? Why is this knowledge important with respect to understanding history?
- How can we trust the fidelity of translations from that original language?

The Eternal Word, God, revealed Himself first through the spoken word, which then became of the written Word, which became the Bible. The Bible is God's book and it presents God's worldview of man. It tells the story of man's original perfection, his rejection of God, and God's plan for redemption that is fulfilled through the Living Word, Jesus Christ. The birth, life, death, and resurrection of Jesus, God's son, is historical fact and the greatest gift bestowed on mankind. It is the central theme of the Bible through all 66 books—books that together comprise an organism throbbing with life, and a system of thinking and understanding.

This historically based system reveals God's perfect plan for restoring His relationship with mankind. It is the lens through which a person develops a Biblical worldview.

> How does the Bible become the lens necessary to develop a Christian or Biblical worldview?

In the Old Testament, God's focus is on Israel but the scope of His purposes encompasses the entire Middle East from Mesopotamia and Egypt to Assyria, to Babylon, to Persia (modern day Iran), to the Greeks and the Romans. In the book of Daniel, we read of Babylonian King Nebuchadnezzar whose dream of these great empires was interpreted by God's servant Daniel. All of these nations were to become realities hundreds of years in the future. Another interesting specific prophecy was made by Isaiah in 605 BC. He wrote that the fortified city of Tyre would be totally destroyed because of its idolatry. The prophecy was so specific that it stated the city would never be rebuilt and that it would only be a place for fisherman to dry their nets. In 580 BC the Babylonians destroyed the land fortress but not the island fortress. In 332 BC, Alexander the Great destroyed the island fortress and today, more than two millennia later, the site of the former is little more than a seaside where fishermen dry their nets. These two examples help affirm that the Bible is God's inspired word because only He knows the future.

> - Why does the Old Testament have a focus on Israel? Does it speak only to its past or also to its future? (A clue: Promises)
> - What other Empires have come and gone since the Roman Empire?

The New Testament includes the historical accounts of the life, teachings, miracles, death and resurrection of Jesus Christ as well as the beginnings of the Christian Church. Jewish historian Josephus (A.D.93) and Roman historian Tacitus (A.D.112) corroborate these Biblical accounts. More than 500 people witnessed Jesus' resurrection. This miraculous historical fact is the foundation of the Christian faith and the basis for a Christian worldview.

> - Why is Jesus' resurrection the foundation of the Christian faith and worldview?
> - Why is it the most significant event in all human history?

As we fast forward to the end of the Bible where we find the Apocalypses (unveilings) of both the books of Daniel and Revelation. These are the revealings of God's plans and purposes regarding: nations, Israel, the church, judgement and end times. For the Christian, history is moving towards a specific climax: the Day of Judgment for nonbelievers and eternity in Heaven for those who trust in Jesus Christ as Lord and Savior. All the other worldviews, including Secular

Humanism, Marxism, and similar 'ism' ideologies, declare that man can save himself by good works and self-sacrifice. The founders of the other ideologies are dead and offer no hope for life beyond the grave! Only through a Biblical worldview do Christians understand true human nature and that it's only through God's Grace that one can be saved and gain eternal life. It is this perspective that enables Christians to view the past, the present and the future through the lens of the Bible to acquire a Biblical worldview.

- Why do Christians say that history is moving to a specific climax and a Day of God's judgment?

- What does this history tell us about God and His Master Plan for human redemption?

- What lessons should individuals and nations have learned from His-Story?

FOR FURTHER DISCUSSION OR PERSONAL REFLECTION:

How does the Bible's linear conception of history help one understand God?

Is there a planned timeline of history? If so, is there a clear beginning and ending to history?

How and where does God disclose his plans and purposes?

How do we know that Jesus was a real historical figure? How does history support our understanding of His resurrection?

Is the Christian church an idea of God or of man? How does it inform a Biblical worldview?

How does a Biblical worldview of history represent reality?

What are the shortcomings of a non-Biblical worldview?

Where does America fit into Bible prophecy?

SESSION 3

WHAT ROLE SHOULD THEOLOGY PLAY IN DEVELOPING A WORLDVIEW?

Throughout the ages, people have tried to understand the basic ideas that are contained in the Biblical story so that they could more easily understand God and live out their daily lives with meaning and purpose. This kind of thinking is called, theology. This term comes from the Greek meaning "God's words" and "reasoning about God." Anytime we talk about God, we are engaged in theology.

Christian theology is the belief in the existence of God as Creator of the universe and all life forms, including human beings. It further declares that God intervenes in His creation by sustaining a personal relationship with his creatures. This theology has two foundational beliefs: (1) special revelation (the Bible) is believed to be God's inspired Word, and (2) general revelation, which is evident in the creation. (Romans 1:20) Christian theology maintains that all history, philosophy, science, mathematics, reasoning and all life experiences confirm the existence of God as the Intelligent Designer, Creator, Redeemer and the sole provider of human salvation from sin and condemnation through faith in Jesus Christ.

- What evidence is there to support the concept of an Intelligent Designer?
- How do we know that the Bible is God's inspired Word?

So, what today makes theology exciting? It is when faith is seeking understanding and finding reality. I realize that few people, although some, will be persuaded to believe in Christ through theological argument. However, for those who believe in Christ or are seeking God, it is important—and exciting—to know that, you don't have to throw your brains out the window to be a Christian. While faith always goes beyond reason and intellect, it is not in opposition to reason and intellect. Throughout history, brilliant scientists, mathematicians, politicians, philosophers, academicians, business and military leaders, and musicians have affirmed their belief in Jesus Christ and his work on the cross.

No faith or religious belief has been more carefully examined and disected, and cross-examined as Christianity. For 2000 years, Christian theology has held its own in the world of ideas. It has stood the test of time! This undertaking is an attempt to understand the sources of Christian belief in the Bible, Christian worship, and Creeds (see appendix) and confessions that have been developed by Christians over the centuries.

However, it is important to remember that the human mind is not capable of adequately understanding or describing God! There is no expression, no combination of expressions, no chapter in any book, including this one, which can begin to do God justice. That's a good thing. Who wants a God who is no bigger than the human mind?

Of course, no theology is adequate unless it illuminates contemporary life and the meaning of Christianity for people in today's world. That's why Christian theology must be continuously studied and evaluated so we can seek to understand as best we can what God chooses to reveal to us. What we think and say about God is not something that we have figured out. It is exploring, embracing and trusting what God has revealed of himself throughout his engagement in history especially as it is recorded in the Old and New Testaments of the Bible.

Christian theology proclaims that God is relational and has a personality characterized by love. He has a master plan which covers the entire span of human history from Creation through Redemption, Salvation, Judgment and Eternity. Believing Christians will spend a lifetime seeking to discover and understand the truths of the Bible. They will read it over and over again allowing it to transform them by the renewing of their minds. They will be conformed to the image of Jesus Christ. That transformation is a lifetime process called sanctification which results in one becoming a 'New Creation' in Christ.

- What is God's Master Plan for humanity?
- Why is God's judgement necessary?

Foundational Christian beliefs are:

1. God is personal and relational and his personality is characterized by love and holiness

2. God reveals himself in three persons, Father, Son and Holy Spirit

3. God has a plan and purpose for each of us and for his creation that is ultimately fulfilled through the life, death and resurrection of Jesus Christ

4. God sent the Holy Spirit to dwell in man while Jesus is in heaven with his father, God

5. Jesus will return to earth as the King of Kings and Lord of Lords to rule the earth from Jerusalem.

> - What difference does it make to you that God, the creator/redeemer loves you and wants to have fellowship with you? (God the Father)
>
> - What difference does it make that Jesus, identified as the Word of God, is God in human form? (God the Son) (John 1:1)
>
> - What difference does it make in your life knowing that God can be with you as the Holy Spirit? (God the Holy Spirit)

Some worldviews in conflict with Christianity begin with, 'in the beginning, no God.' For holders of these worldviews there is no divine image in which we are made; instead, we are seen as no different from the animals, a random evolutionary product of time plus chance. People who espouse these worldviews acknowledge no divine truth to serve as a guide for their lives. They lack an underpinning for their moral decisions and if they acknowledge an afterlife, they are not aware that Heaven is not the default location. They often assume that human nature is good, not sinful, and thus not in need of a redeemer. Whereas the Psalmist (34:6) proclaims, "Oh, taste and see that the Lord is good! Blessed is the man who takes refuge in him!" The atheist worldview believes, "the universe we observe has precisely the properties we should expect if there is at bottom no design, no purpose, no evil, no good, nothing but blind, pitiless indifference." (Richard Dawkins) In other words, for atheists, life has no meaning or purpose and no moral standards. In their minds each of us is our own god.

- What is the likely impact on Society of the inevitable conflict with the Christian worldview?
- Do you believe that Heaven and Hell are real places? Why or why not?

Numerous religions posit a creator God and then define God in human terms often prescribing a set of practices that if followed will protect adherents from calamity or assure them special rewards in an afterlife. These religions often lead individuals to a sense of hopelessness since assurance is based on the impossible task of being perfect. Judaism, Catholicism and Islam are examples of rules-based religions that leave adherents wondering: Did I do enough?

Many other non-Christian ideologies, known as "-isms," are not only different from but actually hostile to the Christian view. Some of the best known are Secular Humanism, Materialism, Naturalism, Marxism/Communism and

Postmodernism. In order for their views to triumph, they have to destroy Christianity or, as seen through history, destroy Christians.

Therefore, to develop a Biblical or Christian worldview, Christians must intentionally study the Bible to understand its truths, to know God, to understand his grace and mercy that led him to send his son, Jesus, to pay the penalty for all of man's sin. Then, he or she must accept Jesus' sacrifice on our behalf. That leads to a personal relationship with Jesus Christ and is the first step in thinking as a Christian.

An important second step is becoming acquainted with the ideologies that are determined to replace a Christian worldview so you can know your enemy and begin putting on the armor of God for protection. (Ephesians 6:11-15) One of the questions for you as a reader of this book is, How will you respond to the challenge presented by Joshua as he led God's chosen people into the "promised land"? "Choose this day whom you will serve . . . But as for me and my house, we will serve the Lord." (Joshua 24:15)

- Which of the 'isms' is the greatest threat to the American republic? Why?
- Why are so many young people in America willing to embrace an 'ism' rather than Christianity?

Another way to gain perspective on the Christian worldview is to explore and understand Christian apologetics—the study and defense of what Christians believe, why they believe it, and why it's important. Apologetics helps individuals understand that Christianity is the only worldview confirmed by reality. Christianity recognizes that humans have a sin nature evident in their propensity for moral corruption, cruelty, dishonesty, wickedness and frequent displays of depravity; sometimes referred to as 'man's inhumanity to man.'

It explains 'what is believed'; including knowledge about God, creation, nature, origins of mankind, sin, morality, stewardship, life's purpose, Jesus Christ, redemption, salvation, heaven, hell, the Christian church, the Bible, the Old Testament history of nations, the end times, judgment and finally, eternity. Old Testament prophecies have proven true such as the one given by the Prophet Daniel, (6th century B.C.), long before the existence of ancient world empires came to be including the Medes and Persians, Greeks and the Romans. There are over 300 prophecies on the first and second coming of Jesus the Messiah; see the Appendix for a short list.

'Why Christians believe it' is rooted in the evidence that the Bible is the divinely inspired Word of God and therefore totally reliable for the truth it proclaims. Christians trust the evidence that proves the Bible is historically correct, the best documented of all ancient books. It also contains prophecy that is 100% accurate because only God can see the future of human history as if it is already completed. (cf, book of Revelation)

> ■ Why is knowing Apologetics important?
> What difference will it make?

Furthermore, as noted in Chapter 2 but worth repeating, the Bible is a miracle in its own right. Written over a period of 1500 years by 40 authors yet without any contradictions. Christians trust and believe the evidence of both Biblical and secular records (Josephus AD 75 & Tacitus AD 116) of the life, teaching, miracles, death by crucifixion, resurrection (witnessed by over 500 people) and Christ's ascension to heaven.

> - What assurance do you have now that verifies the Bible is God's inspired word?
> - Do you believe the Bible is God's operations manual for life? Why or why not?

Christians further believe the evidence of the dramatically transformed lives of Jesus' 11 closest disciples who boldly proclaimed the truth of the gospel and were martyred for their testimonies. The fact is that no one willingly dies or is martyred for what they know to be a lie. Then of course there is the superb contribution of Christianity to western civilization: literature, art, science, music, mathematics, medicine, education, philosophy, and much more including the establishment of our American Republic.

Finally, there is the witness and testimonies of hundreds of millions of followers of Jesus Christ through the centuries. Why so many believers with a Christian view? The answer is because Jesus is the only way to eternal life and a transformed life full of meaning and purpose. He is the way to receive God's gifts of grace, joy, love, peace, forgiveness, contentment, faith and eternal Life.

> - How will embracing Christian Apologetics enable you to be equipped to both contend for and defend your faith?

All the other worldviews and '-isms' present a totally different outlook on humanity none of which is in sync with reality. It's important to remember that the founders of all the other leading worldviews are dead! Only Jesus Christ, who is the foundation of the Christian worldview together with the Bible, is alive and is seated at God's right hand even now. To get a glimpse of Jesus' majesty before his incarnation, see Isaiah 6:1-5. One day he will come back to rule and to reign as King of Kings and Lord of Lords over all creation in a new heaven and a new earth that will be the home of all those who put their faith and trust in Christ as Lord and Savior. In the interim, Jesus calls all of his followers to obey his commandments, love their neighbors and live life guided by a Biblical or Christian worldview.

(Note: For more on Apologetics see the Appendix)

FOR FURTHER DISCUSSION OR PERSONAL REFLECTION:

Why is it important for me to be part of a fellowship of Christ—a church of gathered believers?

Why is it important for me to use my spiritual gifts as part of God's body, the Church?

Why is it important for me to worship God weekly with fellow believers?

Why is it important for me to become and behave like Jesus, live the Christian life?

Why is it important for me to have a daily quiet time with the Lord?

What is the benefit of knowing and memorizing God's promises?

SESSION 4

HOW SHOULD A CHRISTIAN VIEW THE NATURE OF MAN?

The dictionary defines philosophy as the study of the fundamental nature of knowledge, reality and existence, values, reason and the nature of the mind. It is a theory or attitude held by a person, organization or nation that acts as a guiding principle for behavior. Over the centuries, philosophers in pursuit of truth and understanding have examined and challenged almost everything we see around us as well as the ideas that shape societies.

The Greeks were famous for their philosophical approach to life as they spent much time asking and answering questions to discover reality. Some of the well-known names include Aristotle, Epicurus, Plato and Socrates, from whom we get the Socratic method of learning. That method is what we employ in this and our companion study guides—asking and answering profound questions. Jesus was a master of this technique forcing others to think about answers to the very questions they posed to him.

Among the philosophers who have profoundly shaped the thinking of our modern world are St. Augustine of Hippo (c 354-430), St. Thomas Aquinas (c 1224-74), René Descarte (1596-1650), John Locke (1632-1704), David Hume (1711-1776), and Emmanuel Kant (1724-1804).

Philosophers are known not to accept anything as fact unless they can get the logical answers to the profound questions. Some typical questions are, Is there a better way to live? Do humans have free will? Is there life beyond the grave? Why am I here? What is the meaning of life? Does life have a noble purpose? Does God exist? Can God be known? These questions and many others can only be answered with a reasoned or rational Biblical or Christian philosophical worldview.

> How have you sought answers to the above questions?

The Greeks had statues to their many gods including a statue to the, "unknown god." It was the apostle Paul who explained to them that their unknown god is knowable and was the creator of all things and had the answers to all of their questions. Of course, Paul was referring to the God of Creation and the Bible. (Acts 17:22-26) Paul recognized that God was the source of all wisdom and was omniscient.

Just as necessity is referred to as, the mother of invention, and discovery comes about by thinking what no one else has thought, Christianity is in fact, the mother of the scientific method. Christians believe a rational and omniscient God would have created a world governed by principles and laws that are observable and discoverable. That belief continues today as scientists discover more of the mysteries of God.

People today often question how life and the universe began. Many who put their faith in science and history believe that Christians have a non-scientific worldview. However, Christians also believe in science and history BUT they realize that neither science nor history are infallible. Men of science make mistakes, scientific journals may be biased, and history may be distorted to support one view over another. True science and history support the Christian worldview which is actually the most rational of all worldviews. It requires no more faith than any other worldview or philosophy.

- Why is Jesus Christ the most important philosophical truth in the Bible?
- Which is more important, the object of one's faith or the sincerity of it? Why?

For example, many who hold a secular worldview believe that everything began from basic matter or energy and eventually some very elementary form of life happened to generate spontaneously from a primordial soup. That worldview requires faith that "something" always existed but does not explain the origin of that "something." Those who hold that view also believe that the elements got more and more organized until advanced life forms developed. However, the Second Law of Thermodynamics states that there is a natural tendency for isolated systems to degenerate into chaos, not toward more order. Therefore, the secular worldview is in conflict with this scientific law while the Christian worldview is not.

> ■ Which philosophy is more consistent with reality and personal experience, the Christian or worldly materialism? Why?

The secular worldview has faith that a basic life form developed on its own even though intricately designed nucleic acids, lipids, proteins, and carbohydrates are essential components of all known forms of life. The most basic life form is much more complex than a cellphone and a cellphone would certainly not just develop on its own from basic elements. The Christian worldview has faith that a Creator was in charge while designing the universe and creating life.

> ■ Which worldview really requires more faith? Why?

Ultimately, everyone must choose his or her own worldview and this choice will affect every aspect of that individual's life. The Christian worldview is not only supported by honest, scientifically sound truths but also by Biblical revelation. The Gospel of John contains the philosophical foundation of the Christian worldview. It states that in the beginning Jesus already existed. He was with God, and He was God. He created all things and nothing was created without Him. (John 1:1)

The Christian philosophical worldview answers all the profound questions of life's origins, man's purpose, and what happens after we die. This worldview provides a solid rock in a turbulent world of constantly changing opinions and values. A person with a firm Christian worldview will not be tossed to and fro by every secularist doctrine.

- **Do you agree with this last statement? Why?**

FOR FURTHER DISCUSSION OR PERSONAL REFLECTION:

How are our brains and minds different?

Where is your mind? Is it eternal?

What role does your heart play in developing a worldview?

What does supernatural mean?

Does everyone have to choose a worldview?

Is being created in the image of God an important factor in choosing a worldview? Why or why not?

Does a Christian worldview require a rational mind?

Note: Answers to more than 100 profound questions can be found in the book, *Answers to Your Greatest Questions* by Jack Dannemiller, from Living Dialog Ministries.

(Note: See Appendix for more on Man's Noble Purpose)

SESSION 5

HOW DOES UNDERSTANDING THE ORIGINS OF MAN HELP YOU RELATE TO GOD?

In this chapter, we continue our journey to develop a Biblical worldview as we renew our minds with the truth of God and learn to think as a Christian. We will explore two controversial topics that traditionally have appeared as disagreements between science and Christianity. These two topics are from biology and are known as Evolution and the Origin of Man. The Bible does not discuss the subject of evolution. Rather, its worldview assumes God created the world as stated in the book of Genesis. The Biblical worldview of creation is not in conflict with science; rather, it is in conflict with any worldview that starts without a creator, God.

We have seen these two concepts depicted in classrooms and the media as the Darwin chart that illustrates man evolving from monkeys. Now granted many people often act like they are no smarter than a monkey but that is not evidence for the origins of our human species. Also, classrooms show a Tree of Life where animal species are shown to branch off an evolutionary tree at different points suggesting a common ancestor. The tree does not, because it cannot, show how supposed transitions take place.

Most people wrongly assume that science supports evolution, as depicted in that Tree of Life and the Darwin Chart. But science demands that something can only be true until it can be falsified. Darwin himself noted that in the fossil record a sudden presence of a vast variety of complex organisms, (in what is known as the Cambrian explosion) is not explainable by his theory. From the very outset, Darwin's theory of evolution and his companion theory of natural selection was falsified, yet it is still taught in school as if it is scientifically true.

> Why does the theory of evolution (all life springs from a common ancestor) attract so much support even though no scientific evidence has ever been found to support the notion that one species has begotten another?

These laws are so exquisite and precise that many scientists say that an intelligent creator or force was involved. We agree and call him God. He controls the universe and our earth and all the plants and creatures that inhabit it.

So what is true? There is greater evidence of an initial creator who set the universe and the world in motion according to strict laws of physics than there is of all life emerging from a primordial soup in the distant past. The creation speaks of a creator by its beauty and symmetry. "The heavens declare the glory of God and the heavens declare his handiwork." (Psalm 19) The creation reveals itself to have been the work of the wisdom of God in such a way that is rational and comprehensible and reveals itself as a thing of beauty. (Proverbs 8)

The human race has a special place in the plans and providence of God. In some mysterious way, the Spirit of God is within us so that we bear the likeness of God. This identity was to be used by us to steward God's good and perfect creation. (Genesis 1) In the beginning, humans were created to have an uninterrupted fellowship with God, a creature bearing God's likeness and capable of conscious cooperation with God and other human beings. Unfortunately, in the fall, sin entered the world and we lost that capacity with the result that all human beings are self-centered and inclined to take advantage of creation and other human beings including disputes between science and religion.

Science and religion are two related but different domains of human understanding with science answering the question of "How and When" whereas religion answers the question of "Why and for what purpose. "Why" questions cannot be adequately answered by the methods of science unless you are satisfied with the answer, "there is no purpose."

There is "Truth" to be found in both science and religion. So, when searching for "Truth", explore the evidence before drawing conclusions. Don't solely rely on what others say. Especially when it comes to our two big topics, there is a lot of evidence to examine and analyze. This is the challenging and fun part of our journey in developing a Biblical worldview.

> What parts of Darwin's theories regarding the origins of man and natural selection are consistent with creation as posited in the Bible? Which are in conflict?

Do not be troubled by Evolution Theory. Some of it is based on good science. For example, you can accept microevolution for which there is much evidence. It is acceptable to Christians and consistent with the Bible. Microevolution is change over time within a species. For example, there are different breeds of dogs and cats and different kinds of deer, whales, etc. Grape growers for thousands of years have created new varieties through selective cultivation, but to date have not figured out how to get apples to grow on grape vines. Why? Because these changes are not forms of evolution so much as they are adaptations

The second form of evolution postulated by Darwin's tree of life is called macroevolution, or that one species evolves into another species through the process of natural selection. Emerging scientific evidence shows just how problematic embracing this theory has become. No matter where they look, paleontologists and biologists cannot find the theorized transition species. If any exist, they should be in sufficient number and so geographically dispersed as to strongly support evolutionary theory. To date, scientists have only found transitions within a species as described above.

- **Where have scientists looked for evidence of transitional species?**
- **What is your understanding of microevolution?**

Evolution is often presented as a fact based on science, but it is not. It is a theory that has yet to be proven. Although it seemed to make sense back in the time of Charles Darwin in the 19th century, many scientists, even then, challenged his humans were eventually formed. This sounds theoretically possible from a science perspective, but multiple scientific experiments designed to see if this could have happened have all failed. In addition, the statistical probability of it happening is so low as to be declared impossible.

The Scripture model has some scientific merit in that the universe and the earth had a beginning. (Jeremiah 10:12) (Proverbs 8:22-23) This points to something or someone who started it all. The Scripture calls him God. This is also supported scientifically by the precision of life-sustaining natural laws so precise that they could only have come from a creator designer. Chance is ruled out.

Another aspect of creation by a creator is the information that governs the biological process, and there are millions. Examples are the genetic code that produces the 50,000 proteins in the human body, determines enzyme specificity, manages transport of molecules, and guides thousands of other processes. A relatively new term, Intelligent Design, describes these scientific observations because the information is so complex yet so specific. Information could come only from an intelligent designer. This leads to only one conclusion, that God is the giver, designer and sustainer of all life forms, humans included.

> ■ **Could Adam be a historical individual and there still be evolution? If so how?**

Adam is a historic individual from the standpoint that he was created in a moment of time at God's choosing, his presence is documented in the Bible, and he had named descendants confirming Adam's existence.

theories. However Darwin's ideas were embraced by atheists who believed they now had "proof" that there was no God. Evolution provided a way to explain all the animal species and how they grew in number over time, beginning with an initial life form millions of years ago.

That has all changed now with the science of the 20th and 21st centuries. Through science, we now know that our universe had a beginning when some unknown force took an undefined amount of energy and mass and in an instant released it to become all that is known. Unfortunately, as Darwin was in 1850, many of today's scientists cannot or will not try to explain the source of the mass and energy that was released or the force that released it. We have identified that source as God.

We also know that the universe and earth are governed by life-sustaining natural law constants of such precision that they could not have come about by chance. We observe that numerous biological processes appear to operate on incorporated information. Information requires an intelligence. Modern computer and cell phone technology operates on this very principal. Through applied statistics, evolutionary theories on the origins of life and evolution between species are shown to be statistically impossible.

> When it comes to the origin of life which model better aligns with science, a creator God or random selection from nothingness? Why?

The evolutionary model states that initial life formed because of random chemical reactions in a primordial soup of chemicals and then evolved or changed randomly over time into more complex forms until today's modern animals and

Based on Scripture, Adam was created (Genesis 2) separate from the people created in Genesis 1. Adam was God's introductory route into humanity to complete his plan of redemption.

The humans in Genesis 1 were created many thousands of years ago, based on current scientific evidence. Science tells us that they microevolutionary evolved using God-derived processes into the human species God wanted. They were the Homo species. We refer to them sometimes as the human race. Before the creation of the world, Scripture states God had predetermined that humanity would be found holy and blameless in his sight through Jesus Christ. God did exactly that, and the first step was his introduction through Adam. Then there is ample evidence that God seeded his plan with Adam about 7000-10000 years ago and then completed his plan 2000 years ago with the resurrection of Jesus. As a result, we can have a holy and blameless eternal life with Him (Ephesians 1: 4-7).

> How does thinking about human-like species preceding the Biblical Adam affect your understanding of God and the Bible?

All scientists use the same scientific thought processes and apply them using the scientific knowledge of their time. Interestingly, many of the revered scientists of centuries past were Christians. Newton, Boyle, Copernicus, Galileo, Planck, and many others approached their work from a fundamental understanding that natural order derived from a God of creation. When asked why they engaged in scientific study, all said something to the effect that they wanted to see how God did what he did. They saw God behind the science. They were firm believers in God as a wise and rational creator and were amazed at their discoveries that revealed his majesty and power. Their discoveries were the basis for literally every material thing we have today.

> ■ What do you believe is the difference between the early scientists like Newton, Boyle, Copernicus, Galileo, Planck, etc., and many of today's scientists who reject the idea of a Creator God?

You should also know that many great scientists today are Christ-followers. You can be a scientist and a Christian. They see their work the same way as the earlier scientists. Those, who do not accept God as a creator, belong to a group that would worship science as the explanation for everything. Except it cannot. Science is not God!

When we consider developing a worldview on biology and the origins of man, we also need to understand the Anthropic Principle as an argument for God and creation. Simply stated, it is the fine-tuning of the universe to allow life on earth—creation. For decades scientists have been discovering the precise juxtaposition of matter and energy, of protons and neutrons and electrons, of DNA and RNA, of proteins and cells—an incalculable combination of factors that define intelligent life. With each discovery, hundreds of new questions arise and the amazing mystery of human life points more and more to a designer who is beyond human understanding.

Scientists have identified more than 50 characteristics of the universe that must be perfectly balanced to sustain life. Of these, the most sensitive is the space energy density—the self-stretching property of the universe alluded to in the Bible (Psalm 104:2) This property is known as the cosmological constant. In other words, the odds that any given planet in the universe would possess the necessary conditions to support intelligent physical life is one in a number so large it might as well be infinity.

Only an intelligent designer, God, could have created everything necessary for life to exist and flourish on planet earth.

In summary, evolution, as popularly taught today, is in trouble because of the absence of transitional species required to prove evolution, the periodic explosions of life forms without evolvement, and the extreme statistical improbability that chance could be a factor in numerous complex biological processes. A rational mind, renewed by the Scriptures, can easily see a problem in Evolution Theory. In other words, it just requires that you think as a Christian. When you do, you will see that Evolutionary Theory is a religion masquerading as a science. In weighing all the evidence, the scales have tipped in favor of a beginner/creator and an intelligent designer that intentionally made the world and man to occupy it and care for it, God!

It was all done with a purpose. A very noble purpose . . .

For he chose us in him before the creation of the world to be holy and blameless in his sight. In love, He predestined us for adoption to sonship through Jesus Christ, in accordance with his pleasure and will.

Ephesians 1:4-5

(Note: See the Appendix for more on Man's Noble Purpose)

FOR FURTHER DISCUSSION OR PERSONAL REFLECTION:

What mutations have been known to create new species?

Why is the absence of transitional or intermediate forms an argument against evolution?

What scientific evidence is there that design provides a better explanation for life than evolution?

Why is creationism as a worldview for the origins of man untenable for all atheists?

Does belief in evolutionary theory, require more faith than creation by a supernatural God? Why or why not?

SESSION 6

IN WHAT WAY DOES NATURAL AND BIBLICAL LAW PROVIDE A FOUNDATION FOR A CHRISTIAN WORLDVIEW?

Many people are under the misconception that the Bible has little to say about law beyond the 10 Commandments. In this chapter we will explore a Christian worldview of both natural law and Biblical law. A Christian understands how law plays a part in the world that God created. This understanding forms part of a Christian's worldview, renewing our minds with the truth of God's Word.

There are two important factors in understanding law: (1) man's moral worth; and (2) man's rebellious nature. Man has worth. Man was created by God in the image and likeness of God. Thus, there is an inherent value in a person. That worth is not earned but is given in man's creation. It is often called "moral worth" or "the dignity of man." Thus, to harm or murder a man is to deny him the value and dignity bestowed upon him by God.

Also, man has a rebellious nature. Man disobeyed God and the result was a change in man's nature. His nature became self-centered. As such, man will devise ways to achieve his own self-interests, often harming others. Law attempts to control this rebellion in man.

> ■ What controls are necessary in society to dissuade individuals from breaking the law?

Because of these two factors, moral worth and rebelliousness, God has given two types of law: (1) natural law; and (2) Biblical law.

Natural Law. Man, whether Christian or not, has a conscience. The conscience includes a memory bank of rules governing right and wrong. Man is born with these rules. As man acts, his conscience views this memory bank, and signals to the man whether he should or should not carry out the action. It is an inherent sense of right and wrong. It is called natural law. Thus, all individuals are held accountable to God for their actions in abiding by or disobeying the built-in understanding of right or wrong known as conscience.

Many cultures, including Judaism and Christianity, summarize this law as the Golden Rule: Do unto others as you would have others do unto you.

> ■ How does the conscience play an important role in developing a Biblical worldview?

The signers of America's Declaration of Independence referred to the Laws of Nature and Nature's God and proclaimed that all men are created equal and are endowed by their Creator with certain unalienable Rights. They concluded by appealing to the Supreme Judge of the world firmly relying on the protection of divine Providence.

All of the men who gathered in Philadelphia in 1776, identified themselves as Christians, and were well acquainted with the Bible, They "believed in and based the nation's independence on Natural Law; that is, that God in creating the universe, implanted in the nature of man a body of Law to which all human beings are subject, which is superior to all manmade law and which is knowable by human reason."*

The nation's founders tied their understanding of Natural Law to a set of God-given rights later codified in the Constitution and, in particular, the first 10 amendments. Those rights come under the broad headings of Life, Liberty and the pursuit of Happiness.

> ▪ I what ways has the understanding of Natural Law by America's Founding Fathers influenced this nation?

Biblical Law. In addition to Natural Law, through his word, the Bible, God has provided a framework for living in relationship with Him, with our families and with all other humans. The intent of Biblical Law is not only to protect man, but keep him on a right path that provides a healthy, blessed and happy life.

. . . *happy is he who keeps the law.*

Proverbs 29:18.

---

* Barker, Robert's. *"Natural Law and the United States Constitution."* The Review of Metaphysics (Nov. 2012)

Blessed is the one
  who does not walk in step with the wicked
or stand in the way that sinners take
  or sit in the company of mockers,
but whose delight is in the law of the Lord,
  and who meditates on his law day and night..

Psalm 1:1-2.

Biblical Law and Natural Law are beautifully summed up by Jesus when he was asked by one of the great Bible scholars of his day, "What is the greatest commandment?"

Jesus replied: "'Love the Lord your God with all your heart and with all your soul and with all your mind.' This is the first and greatest commandment. And the second is like it: 'Love your neighbor as yourself.' All the Law and the Prophets hang on these two commandments."

Matthew 22:36-40

In addition to God's law that is burned onto the hearts and minds of men (Natural Law) and made evident through God's word (Biblical Law), man creates civil law. Man realizes that laws are required to temper the natural instincts of men and women. These laws are usually designed to protect individuals from harmful actions of others and to make individuals accountable for their actions. However, civil laws may not conform to God's Biblical Law, and in fact may contradict both Natural and Biblical Law. Such contradictory laws are often established based on selfish desires of man.

> What civil laws contradict Natural and Biblical Law? How have they helped or harmed individuals or society as a whole?

As a citizen we have a responsibility to uphold the law. That's why a Christian ought to spend time learning God's Law—Natural and Biblical—to better understand the mind of God. After all, the results of learning and applying God's Law are a fruitful and prosperous life.

> *That person is like a tree planted by streams of water,*
>   *which yields its fruit in season*
> *and whose leaf does not wither—*
>   *whatever they do prospers.*
>
> Psalm 1:3.

> *My son, do not forget my teaching,*
>   *but keep my commands in your heart,*
> *for they will prolong your life many years*
>   *and bring you peace and prosperity.*
>
> Proverbs 3:1-2

Law that follows Biblical principles protects each of us and the ones we love. God's law is true. It is designed to increase the happiness of everyone, ensuring a fair and just society when it is obeyed.

> Given the preceding concepts and Scripture references, how should law figure into a Christian's worldview?

FOR FURTHER DISCUSSION OR PERSONAL REFLECTION:

If God's law is to increase my happiness, why is it broken so often?

What is wrong with the world and what are the symptoms? What is the remedy?

Who is the righteous king who will one day rule over all the earth and end injustice?

Why can't the world clean up its mess until the righteous king arrives?

SESSION 7

HOW SHOULD A BIBLICAL UNDERSTANDING OF MARRIAGE AND FAMILY GUIDE A CHRISTIAN'S WORLDVIEW?

Family is God's basic building unit for a fair, safe, happy and just society. It is in the family where parents teach children moral values, right and wrong, to be responsible for their behavior and decisions and to experience trust and love and obedience to the parents and to God's precepts. It is in a family where the first Biblical worldview's are encountered and passed along. A worldview, as we have seen in previous sessions, is an intellectual, emotional, and spiritual filter that people acquire over time. It helps them to experience, interpret, and respond to everything that happens in their lives. It becomes their reality check of the culture in which they live.

"A person's worldview starts developing at 15 to 18 months of age and is almost completely formed by age 13. We refine that worldview during our teens and early 20s and figure out how to best implement it and articulate it. It's our way of trying to understand, 'how did Jesus think?' This filter causes us to act in response to stimuli in particular ways. You might want to think like Jesus so that you can act like Jesus. For someone who is a follower of Christ that would be their thought process."*

* George Barna, Senior Research Fellow at the Center for Biblical Worldview, in an interview in *Faith, Family Freedom*, Fall 2021

> ■ What is the parent's role in shaping their children's worldview?
>
> ■ What can the Christian Church do to equip the parents for this challenge?

A survey of more than 1000 American adults conducted by George Barna, of the Family Research Council's Center for Biblical Worldview showed that 51% claim to have a Biblical worldview but in fact just 6% actually do. The reality is that with each succeeding generation in America the Biblical worldview is on the decline. Only 2% of the children of millennials are found to have a Biblical worldview. If this trend is not reversed, then society in America will experience even greater chaos than is present today.

> ■ What has contributed to this decline in the number of Americans who hold a Biblical worldview?

Against the sobering statistics shown above, let's look at how one comes to an understanding of and gains a Biblical perspective on marriage and family. Thinking as a Christian in the realm of marriage and family may be the most important part of a Biblical worldview. Apart from money, Jesus spoke more about familial relationships than with any other subject.

Marriage and family life are central themes of the Bible beginning with the first family, continuing through Noah, Abraham, Moses, Joshua, David and Solomon and on into the family of Jesus.

So the Lord God caused the man to fall into a deep sleep; and while he was sleeping, he took one of the man's ribs and then closed up the place with flesh. Then the Lord God made a woman from the rib he had taken out of the man, and he brought her to the man. The man said,

"This is now bone of my bones
　　and flesh of my flesh;
she shall be called 'woman,'
　　for she was taken out of man."

That is why a man leaves his father and mother and is united to his wife, and they become one flesh.

Genesis 1:21-24

- Why did God create marriage?
- How is marriage defined in the Bible? How is that the same as or different from society's definition?

The Bible documents families with genealogies being central to the fulfillment of prophecies from the time that God promised to make Abram, a 75 year-old man with no children, the father of a great nation. (Genesis 12) Abram's wife, Sarai, who had been childless for decades conceives and bears a son 25 years later when she is 90 and thought to be past child bearing. (Genesis 21)

The Biblical narrative follows the story of Abraham and his descendants through their many joys and sorrows and the consequences of failing to live up to their side of the covenant with God. Like a parent, God continuously shows his love for his people even as he disciplines them for disobeying his commands—commands that were given to establish a fair and just society and to ensure that healthy families were at the heart of community life. These commands included:

You shall have no other gods before me.

Honor your father and your mother, so that you may live long in the land the Lord your God is giving you.

You shall not commit adultery.

You shall not covet your neighbor's house. You shall not covet your neighbor's wife, or his male or female servant, his ox or donkey, or anything that belongs to your neighbor.

Exodus 20:3,12,14,17

To reinforce the commands, God, through Moses instructed the people further:

Fix these words of mine in your hearts and minds; tie them as symbols on your hands and bind them on your foreheads. Teach them to your children, talking about them when you sit at home and when you walk along the road, when you lie down and when you get up. Write them on the doorframes of your houses and on your gates, so that your days and the days of your children may be many in the land the Lord swore to give your ancestors, as many as the days that the heavens are above the earth.

Deuteronomy 11:18-21

When a husband and wife are in a right relationship with God and each other, their families will flourish. Through the structure of the family, God provides on earth a representation of God as father—one who is to be revered and respected. Though imperfect, fathers have a unique role in the family that of representing to their children what a loving God does for them. He is responsible for protecting, and providing and ensuring that his children are trained both in God's commands and in life skills. Likewise, mothers have the important role of nurturing their children and serving as a counterbalance to their husbands.

> - **What happens to society when people disregard God's command with respect to adultery?**
> - **How does the diligent teaching of God's commands to children help create a flourishing society?**

The Bible is unique in ancient literature insofar as it does not sanitize the lives of its "heroes." The flaws are not glossed over, but are shown to provide cautionary tales for those of us who read the stories. King David, who is described as a man after God's own heart, did not live a sinless life. On the contrary, he arranged for the death of man so he might have the man's wife. David's son, Solomon, despite gaining the reputation of being the wisest man ever, was very unwise with respect to raising his own sons. This is ironic, because we still read today, these words he penned 3,000 years ago.

Start children off on the way they should go,
  and even when they are old they will not turn from it.

Proverbs 22:6

The result of Solomon not heeding his own words, was a rivalry among his sons, the splitting of his kingdom and eventually the destruction of the Jewish nation. This came about because his sons and many kings who followed them turned away from God and ignored the commands that God gave to the people as part of his covenant with them.

> - **What happens to families when fathers are absent physically, emotionally or spiritually?**
> - **How should the church address this challenge?**

The Old Testament concludes with the prophetic book of Malachi, and it is here we get one of the best pictures of God's reason for marriage and its importance. God, speaking through the prophet, points out how unfaithfulness to each other is an assault on God's desire for husbands and wives. This unfaithfulness causes a separation not only between the man and woman, but between them and God, as well.

You weep and wail because he (God) no longer looks with favor on your offerings or accepts them with pleasure from your hands. You ask, "Why?" It is because the Lord is the witness between you and the wife of your youth.

You have been unfaithful to her, though she is your partner, the wife of your marriage covenant. Has not the one God made you? You belong to him in body and spirit. And what does the one God seek? Godly offspring. So be on your guard, and do not be unfaithful to the wife of your youth. "The man who hates and divorces his wife, says the Lord Almighty, "does violence to the one he should protect,"

So be on your guard, and do not be unfaithful.

Malachi 2:13-16

In the New Testament, Jesus cites the Old Testament Scriptures when talking about the importance of the marriage covenant to Pharisees. These were very devout Jews who not only memorized all of the first five books of the Old Testament, but also scrupulously tried to live by their understanding of the law given to Moses.

Some Pharisees came to him to test (Jesus). They asked, "Is it lawful for a man to divorce his wife for any and every reason?"

"Haven't you read," he replied, "that at the beginning the Creator 'made them male and female,' and said, 'For this reason a man will leave his father and mother and be united to his wife, and the two will become one flesh'? So they are no longer two, but one flesh. Therefore what God has joined together, let no one separate."

"Why then," they asked, "did Moses command that a man give his wife a certificate of divorce and send her away?"

Jesus replied, "Moses permitted you to divorce your wives because your hearts were hard. But it was not this way from the beginning. I tell you that anyone who divorces his wife, except for sexual immorality, and marries another woman commits adultery."

Matthew 19:3-9

- How should God's emphasis on faithfulness affect how we think, act and interact with those who reject God's authority?

- Jesus reminds the Pharisees of God's plan to create humans as males and females. How should that statement from the co-creator inform our understanding of genders?

Since we live in an imperfect world, Christians must make some accommodation for situations that are not consistent with God's commands. Paul the Apostle in writing to the Church in Corinth provides a framework for such accommodation.

To the married I give this command (not I, but the Lord): A wife must not separate from her husband. But if she does, she must remain unmarried or else be reconciled to her husband. And a husband must not divorce his wife.

To the rest I say this (I, not the Lord): If any brother has a wife who is not a believer and she is willing to live with him, he must not divorce her. And if a woman has a husband who is not a believer and he is willing to live with her, she must not divorce him. For the unbelieving husband has been sanctified through his wife, and the unbelieving wife has been sanctified through her believing husband. Otherwise your children would be unclean, but as it is, they are holy.

But if the unbeliever leaves, let it be so. The brother or the sister is not bound in such circumstances; God has called us to live in peace. How do you know, wife, whether you will save your husband? Or, how do you know, husband, whether you will save your wife? Nevertheless, each person should live as a believer in whatever situation the Lord has assigned to them, just as God has called them.

I Corinthians 7:10-17

In another letter, this one to the church in Ephesus, Paul sums up the Biblical view of marriage in a powerful, positive way:

Wives, submit yourselves to your own husbands as you do to the Lord. For the husband is the head of the wife as Christ is the head of the church, his body, of which he is the Savior. Now as the church submits to Christ, so also wives should submit to their husbands in everything.

Husbands, love your wives, just as Christ loved the church and gave himself up for her to make her holy, cleansing her by the washing with water through the word, and to present her to himself as a radiant church, without stain or wrinkle or any other blemish, but holy and blameless. In this same way, husbands ought to love their wives as their own bodies. He who loves his wife loves himself. After all, no one ever hated their own body, but they feed and care for their body, just as Christ does the church—for we are members of his body. "For this reason a man will leave his father and mother and be united to his wife, and the two will become one flesh." This is a profound mystery—but I am talking about Christ and the church. However, each one of you also must love his wife as he loves himself, and the wife must respect her husband.

Ephesians 5:21-30

- **What tools has God given to the Christian to help him or her deal with challenging situations in marital relationships?**

- **How do the admonitions for wives to submit and husbands to love resonate among modern readers?**

- **Why might some people say the Bible is old and out of step with the realities of today's culture?**

- **How is today's cultural understanding of relationships between men and women helping or hurting our society?**

FOR FURTHER DISCUSSION OR PERSONAL REFLECTION:

How should we raise children so that their lives reflect the love, compassion, and glory of God?

How can we help bring healing to broken marriages and broken families?

What price is our society paying for turning its back on God and his plan for faithful, successful marriages?

"Honor your father and your mother, so that you may live long in the land the Lord your God is giving you."

Why is this commandment the only one that includes a promise?

How has the breaking of this commandment affected not only families, but schools and civil society?

SESSION 8

HOW DO GOVERNMENT AND POLITICS INFLUENCE THE LIFE OF A CHRISTIAN?

In Session 6 on Law, we laid down the foundation for government and politics, because once law is codified someone must take responsibility to ensure the laws are followed. That is the role of government. Politics is the human element of deciding who will be charged with oversight of the law.

As we discuss government and politics you are likely to discover a bumpy ride on our journey to renew our minds by the truth of God's Word. Fine tuning our Biblical worldview in this arena will be challenging.

Politics has been a part of the human experience for thousands of years. Governing a nation or leading a family inevitably leads to establishing a set of rules or laws ideally for the benefit and protection of the citizens and family members. One of the earliest structures for government was put in place by Moses at the suggestion of his father-in-law, Jethro (Exodus 18:20-23). The key was to select individuals who were competent, who feared God, and were persons of truth, not given to covetousness. These qualities would help to assure wise counsel and justice for all. These simple standards should be primary in selecting and voting for candidates running for office today. That is a Biblical worldview.

> **How should a Christian worldview inform your selection of office holders at the national, state and local level?**

As we shall see, there is a wide range of structures for government and politics, but not all are equally beneficial or just. The Bible, however, does have the worldview that is preferred by God. So, let's consider the possibilities in the first segment and the key questions that are presented for discussion.

"Human government was instituted by God to protect man's unalienable rights from mankind's sinful tendencies." (*Thinking Like a Christian,* David Noebel) It became necessary because of the fall and disobedience of Adam and Eve. Since all persons are inherently sinful, their evil inclinations must be kept in check by laws and by government capable of enforcing such laws. For this reason, the Bible advocates limited power in the government, something between totalitarianism on the one hand and anarchy on the other.

To disperse power, our republic has divided federal government into three branches—legislative, executive and judicial—with a system of what are known as checks and balances. Political power is further dispersed below the federal level into state and local governments. In summary, the state is a God-ordained institution with God-ordained limitations.

- Why did God institute human government?
- What kind of government does the Bible advocate, and why?
- How is power supposed to be dispersed in the system of government codified in the United States Constitution?

Our nation's founding document, the Declaration of Independence (1776), states: "We hold these truths to be self-evident, that all men are created equal, that they are endowed by their Creator with certain unalienable rights, that among these are Life, Liberty and the pursuit of Happiness.– That to secure these rights, governments are instituted among Men, deriving their just powers from the consent of the governed." This brilliant insight testifies to the Founders' belief that our rights come from God, not from government. This conviction was repeated later by President John F. Kennedy: "The rights of man come not from the generosity of the state but from the hand of God."

This understanding was central to the U.S. Constitution drafted in 1789. As to the form of government, ideas popularized in both Greek and Roman cultures before the birth of Christ, were introduced. It was Benjamin Franklin who, when leaving the constitutional convention, was asked, "Doctor, what have we got? A republic or a monarchy?" His response was, "a Republic, if you can keep it!" He, no doubt, was reflecting on the failures of republics in Greece and Rome, and almost 2000 years of history when totalitarian governments were the rule and individuals enjoyed few rights.

That's what makes the American experiment unique in world history. Here is a nation that was founded on the notion that man was created by a supernatural Being; second, this Being, God alone, is the bestower of human rights. The first 10 amendments to the Constitution are collectively known as the Bill of Rights. These are not rights granted by the government (or some monarch) that can be taken away at the whim of a man-made institution, but rather they are God-given rights that the Government must not abridge.

> - In what sense is everyone "created equal"?
> - Why are governments "instituted among men"?
> - What is the Bill of Rights?
> - When developing a Christian worldview, how should an individual view the American republican form of government?

Another key function of government—besides protecting man's God-given rights—is to administer justice, i.e. the practice of truth in human relationships . . . and rendering to each his due according to a right standard. Thus, "promoting justice" becomes more important than any other aspect of government. When government oversteps its bounds—specifically when it tries to usurp God's sovereignty—utopianism and totalitarianism are the result.

Abandoning God and placing trust in an individual or in the state will always result in a power-mad and abusive state. As William Penn said, "If we are not governed by God, then we will be ruled over by tyrants."

> - What does tyranny look like?
> - What is a Christian's role in preventing or opposing tyranny?

The atrocities of the Soviet Union under Joseph Stalin or Nazi Germany under Adolf Hitler were the results of tyrants seizing control of nations. Ironically, these men were initially lauded by individuals who had the misplaced hope that they and their governments would someday create a perfect environment and perfect human beings. Sadly, these ideas about utopian government have not gone away. They just surface under different labels such as "Socialism," "Democratic Socialism," and "Progressivism," promoting so-called social justice. In Session 10, we will explore the concept of social justice in more detail.

> - What are the keys to successful government that both protects rights and dispenses justice?
> - How do politicians try to usurp God's sovereignty? What's the result?
> - What are the barriers to a state creating the perfect environment for human life?

We read in Romans 13:1, "Let every person be subject to the governing authorities, for there is no authority except from God, and those that exist have been instituted by God." Thus, the Christian is called to obey the government, to honor justice and to preserve order. This includes voting, running for office, serving in non-elected offices, being appointed to local school boards, and, if politics goes against God's truth, attempting to correct the deviance. Still, when God's commands conflict with those of the state, the Christian has the right, even the duty, to remain obedient to God, no matter the consequences.

Think of Daniel opting for a death in the lions' den rather than worshiping King Nebuchadnezzar. (Daniel 6) Also recall the three men named Shadrach, Meshach, and Abednego who refused to worship the king's golden image and were thrown into the fiery furnace, rather than deny God. (Daniel 3) Remember too that the Apostles continued to preach Jesus even in the face of persecution and death by the Roman government. In Mark 12:16 Jesus gave us a clear, simple illustration of obeying the civil government: "Give unto Caesar what is Caesar's; and unto God what is God's."

- How should Christians respond to governing authorities?
- What lessons can we learn from Daniel's disobedience of the law set forth by King Nebuchadnezzar?
- What are a Christian's options when God's commands conflict with those of the state?

We conclude this session remembering that the Christian's worldview must be based on God's Biblical truth and that a believer must remain obedient to God always and in all circumstances. What is important is faithfulness, not necessarily the success of one's efforts.

- What key principles of the Christian or Biblical worldview most help you keep a balanced view towards government and politics?

FOR FURTHER DISCUSSION OR PERSONAL REFLECTION:

What is Utopianism? How does it conflict or align with a Biblical worldview of government and politics?

How does man's obedience to the law keep the need for governmental power at a minimum?

Whom do we obey when God's commands conflict with those in authority?

Can you think of other episodes in the Bible where conflict with governing authority ensued for the person involved? What were they?

What did Jesus promise the Holy Spirit would do if Christians were brought unjustly before the state. Why is that important? (See Mark 13:11.)

SESSION 9

HOW DOES A BIBLICAL WORLDVIEW HELP YOU EVALUATE COMPETING ECONOMIC SYSTEMS?

Many believe that the study of the workings of an economy belong in university business schools. However, since humans are impacted every day by the economic culture of their nation state, i.e. the need for 'daily bread', clothing, shelter, employment, etc., each has a worldview, whether they realize it or not. They instinctively understand the law of supply and demand for the goods and services they need to live. History has shown that some economic systems work better than others.

> What role should the church play in educating its members about economic systems?

While we will explore some of the features, benefits and limitations of those economic systems, our focus is on these four questions:
Does the Bible have anything to say about economics? Has God provided a set of principles that would point to one system being better than another?

Is it important to embrace a Biblical worldview about economics?

Can thinking like a Christian about economics impact the choices we make about the following;

- Discovering your life calling
- Embracing a Christian work ethic
- Stewarding God's resources
- Making wise investments
- Working for a noble cause
- Practicing morality in business—The Golden Rule
- Taking risk—personal and financial
- Exercising social responsibility with respect to individuals, families, community, the nation, and the world.
- Achieving profit, wealth, security, eternal rewards.

Christians do not necessarily all agree on one best worldview of economics. The Bible declares that man is sinful by nature and therefore does not always act in the best interest of all. Therefore some form of government and related economic system is necessary to oversee man's inherent nature. So which economic system best aligns with Biblical principles? The economic systems at play in the world today fall between communism and laissez-faire capitalism. In each, the government plays a role, though to what degree varies widely.

Let's start with the basics. Christians know that God decreed through the Apostle Paul that, "The one who is unwilling to work shall not eat." (2 Thessalonians 2:10) This command has become known as the Christian work ethic. That command to work also came directly from God to Adam in the Garden of Eden. (Genesis 2:15) The implied benefit of one's work is the right to own the property that yielded the food. That property has been defined through history as the land and tools, as well as the mental and physical effort brought by an individual to a particular task.

> - How should work be defined in our 21st-century world?
> - When property is defined as being more than land or possessions, how does that affect your understanding of work?

The Bible endorses the concept of justice under the law because God is just. However, no man-made system is fully just and man's inherently self-centered nature leads many to try and take what belongs to another. Sometimes the taking is by one person from another, but most usually it is a collective taking by a government to improve the lives of others. While that taking may result in improved living and working conditions, often the improvements are in the lives of a few who are favored by the government.

Free enterprise economies where government interference is limited people tend to act responsibly and to make wise choices. As government interference increases through laws, regulations and taxes, individuals and businesses often are forced to make decisions that may not be in their best interests or in the best interests of their families, customers, suppliers, investors or the community as a whole.

In his vision of a "New Jerusalem" the prophet Isaiah sees an ideal, God-ordained future, that looks a lot more like a capitalist rather than a socialist one. Here people will finally get to enjoy their property without the fear of someone taking it away from them.

> They will build houses and dwell in them; they will plant
> vineyards and eat their fruit.
> No longer will they build houses and others live in them, or
> plant and others eat.
> For as the days of a tree, so will be the days of my people; my
> chosen ones will long enjoy the work of their hands.
> They will not labor in vain, nor will they bear children doomed
> to misfortune;
> for they will be a people blessed by the Lord, they and their
> descendants with them.
>
> Isaiah 65:21-23

- What are the benefits and drawbacks of allowing individuals to be solely responsible for their economic decisions?
- Why might checks and balances be necessary in an economic system? What role should government play?

Let's take a closer look at the principles that undergird the two economic theories most often at work in the world today: capitalism and socialism. Under which system are individuals most likely to thrive? Which is more likely to allow religious freedom to be enjoyed? Which best embraces God's charge to Adam to take care of the earth? Answering these questions are foundational to a Christian's worldview

One distinguishing and important feature of capitalism is economic freedom. It is concerned with the free and voluntary and peaceful exchange of goods and services influenced by the forces of supply and demand. Socialism by contrast seeks to replace freedom in the marketplace by central bureaucratic government planners who exercise control over market functions. Unfortunately, many of the bureaucrats who believe they have superior knowledge as to how markets should work discover too late that their ideas do not comport with reality. As they try to manage major systems within an economy including financial, energy, healthcare, and education the utopia they pursue always fails to materialize. Venezuela, Russia, Cuba and other countries that have embraced socialism/communism demonstrate the inadequacy of centrally planned bureaucratic economies. Without the opportunity for direct benefit, working under socialism has been described by one who fled its yoke as follows: "we pretended to work, and they pretended to pay us."

By contrast, free enterprise capitalism has demonstrated success in improving societies in which it has been employed. That's because the success of the entrepreneur is dependent on the success of a wide range of stakeholders including owners, customers, employees, suppliers, the local community, governments, society and, for Christians, God.

> - How does a system that allows individuals the freedom to succeed or fail benefit society as a whole?
> - What lessons learned from failure enable a person to achieve great things for God and mankind?
> - What are the drawbacks to allowing people to fail?

There are a number of examples in Scripture supporting the ownership and stewardship of private property including many of Jesus' parables. Even in describing his return to earth at the end of time, Jesus alludes to the importance of wise stewardship of property. (Matthew 25:14-28)

The right to property ownership results from man's duty to work for a living. There are also many Proverbs which support the concept that diligent work brings prosperity. With the right to own property comes the responsibility to be a faithful steward of God's resources. Since God owns everything, the steward seeks to maximize the return on investment and use that success to honor God by serving others in need, i.e. Christian charity. The Bible affirms the principle that Christians are to take care of widows and orphans and those who through no fault of their own find themselves in need. (James 1:27) It is the responsibility of both individual believers and the Christian church. The Bible never said that the government should replace Christian charity.

- How do Biblical references to work and ownership of private property comport with references to helping the poor, caring for the sick, protecting widows and orphans, and welcoming aliens?
- How are individuals accountable to God for the way in which they use property and care for those in need?

In the free enterprise system, economic competition is encouraged. Citizens in a free-market society can produce goods and services using their God-given creativity to meet or create a market need producing something of value for others. Individuals can voluntarily exchange their time and abilities (work) to secure property (paycheck) that they in turn can use for their personal betterment and for the betterment of their families and communities. Profit from a free market system enables individuals the privilege of contributing to the welfare of society in a way that preserves each person's dignity and pride.

> - How do these ideas of competition and individuality fit into a Christian worldview?
> - In what ways does capitalism enhance a society? In what ways might it negatively impact God's creation?
> - In what ways does socialism enhance a society? In what ways might it negatively impact God's creation?

In the free enterprise Capitalist system individuals can select their field of work based on their individual talents, spiritual gifts and interests. In Socialism opportunities for education and employment are frequently dictated by the bureaucratic establishment based on what seems right to the bureaucrat not necessarily on market needs or the needs and desires of the individuals they purport to serve.

A Capitalistic economic system depends upon the premise of equal opportunity not a guarantee of equal outcomes. By contrast, a Socialistic economic system operates on the principal of equity or equal outcomes for all.

When Moses was telling people about God's law and how it should be applied in the Promised Land into which they were entering, he warned them:

There will always be poor people in the land. Therefore I command you to be openhanded toward your fellow Israelites who are poor and needy in your land.

Deuteronomy 15:11

Jesus referenced this command when he called out the disciples who were offended that a woman was "wasting" expensive perfume that could be sold to help the poor. He reminded them that there will always be poor people so long as men turn from their worship of God. (Matthew 26:11) God had planned on there being no poor in Israel so long as his people remained faithful to him.

In a world in which billions have turned their back on God, there will always be both rich and poor. It is not a sin to be successful and to become wealthy provided that one's economic success is based on the Golden Rule and used to invest in building God's kingdom (not one's own) and to be charitable.

Nor is it a sin to be poor. In his book, *Thinking Like a Christian*, David Noebel quotes author and philosophy professor Ronald Nash saying, "It is certainly true, that Scripture recognizes that poverty sometimes results from exploitation. But Scripture also teaches that there are times when poverty results from misfortunes that have nothing to do with exploitation. These misfortunes include accidents, injuries, and illness. And of course the Bible also makes it plain that poverty can result from indigence and sloth or laziness." There can also be significant structural shifts to new technologies and industries that can cause unemployment and poverty for some who can't adapt.

When one group of people believe that they can plan an economy better than the market, (socialism) they usually begin by advocating control of small parts of the economy in the interest of fairness. Soon they seek control over worker pay and benefits, prices of goods and services, means of production and wealth accumulation. To manage all of this a central government grows larger and evermore powerful, using political power, coercion, and eventually police or military force to ensure compliance with the many rules and regulations necessary to oversee key elements of the economy.

By contrast, free enterprise allows citizens to determine what profession they will choose, how they will spend their money, and how they will use their resources for their personal needs and the betterment of society.

> How does real-world understanding of economic systems help you form your Christian worldview?

Some Christians suggest that after Pentecost, when the new Christians in Jerusalem shared everything they had in common they were involved in God-sanctioned socialism. (Acts 2: 42-47) However a careful reading shows that those who were accepting Jesus Christ as their Savior and Lord were acting out of gratefulness and love on a personal level (not government coercion) to ensure that all were cared for. Since many of the new Christians were in Jerusalem for the celebration of Pentecost, they may not have been prepared for an extended stay, and needed food, clothes and shelter. If anything, this passage reinforces the notion that free people, acting freely to use their property for the betterment of others closely aligns with Biblical teaching about economics.

FOR FURTHER DISCUSSION OR PERSONAL REFLECTION:

What does the Bible have to say about risk-taking or use of talents?

How should educators be equipped to guide students in an understanding of economic systems while providing learning experiences that will enable individuals to discover their God-given gifts, and to find a noble purpose for work that honors God?

Why do free market economies ensure that the wealthy create more wealth for themselves as well as for others?

In what ways do you agree or disagree with this statement: *Capitalism encourages freedom in the market and in the political sphere. It removes the danger of granting excess sovereignty to the state instead of God.*

After carefully considering the alternatives, which economic system best aligns with a Biblical or Christian worldview?

SESSION 10

HOW DOES A CHRISTIAN VIEW OF SOCIAL JUSTICE MESH WITH A SECULAR VIEW?

Social justice is rooted in the Bible, particularly in the teachings of Jesus. He embraced the marginalized, healed the sick, and reminded people of the Golden Rule, to do unto others as you would want them to do to you. Recently, the term social justice has taken on a new or expanded meaning on the political and cultural scene. Certainly the idea of social justice, seems noble and appealing. However, Christians would be wise to compare the Bible's view of social justice with that of many political, community, business and church leaders.

The Social Justice Movement (SJM) in many churches—particularly mainline protestant and catholic—seems to focus on meeting the physical needs of mankind by ensuring equal access to food, healthcare, employment opportunities, and housing…and ensuring acceptance of all people as they are. In society as a whole, SJM seems also to embrace the notion that more than just equality of opportunities and a legal system that ensures equal treatment of all, society should ensure equitable outcomes citing disparities in wealth accumulation, rates of incarceration, healthcare, housing, educational achievement, and representation in government.

The SJM influence can be seen in calls to tax the rich, provide universal healthcare and free education, cancel loans and end local zoning. Other SJM initiatives call for removing restrictions on immigration and giving reparations to victims of policies that harmed certain groups of people.

Given Biblical commands to feed the hungry, clothe the poor, care for widows and orphans shouldn't everyone wants social justice? The United States Constitution enshrines the concepts of equality under the law, so only when looking at how the SJM frames its arguments can we begin to discover ideas that may be inconsistent with both the Bible and our civil laws.

The concept of social justice today has become a catchphrase for the redistribution of wealth, elimination of educational and employment standards, reduction in law enforcement and equality of compensation regardless of education or skills or competency and granting special privileges to individuals who are identified as minorities (political, ethnic, religious, gender, etc.) within a nation.

> What is your concept or idea of Social Justice? How does that square with your understanding of Biblical teaching?

The Scales of Justice Figure is a blindfolded woman holding scales and a sword to affirm the principle that under the law each individual is viewed as equal to all others. This imagery was introduced by the Roman Emperor Augustus more than 2,000 years ago, but is based on a similar depiction of an ancient Egyptian goddess of justice. The Bible also reminds us that God is not a respecter of persons and neither is the law.

God, as the supreme judge of the universe, treats each person equally according to his laws and principles.

In his book, *We Will Not Be Silenced: Responding with Courage to Our Culture's Assault on Christianity*, pastor, broadcaster and author Erwin Lutzer writes, "A just law is a man-made code that squares with the moral law or the law of God." One day, all humans who have ever lived will stand before God to give an accounting of their lives not against man's standards, but against God's moral law.

> When giving account of their lives before God, are people more apt to plead for justice or mercy? Why?

God sees and judges people as individuals. He does not define people according to the nationality, ethnicity, or other social group into which they may be identified by man. Purveyors of social justice seek to lump people into categories and prescribe outcomes for all members of those categories regardless of personal interests, abilities, gifts, capacities, work ethics, values, education, upbringing, willingness to sacrifice, degrees of courage, ability to defer gratification or their stations in life.

> How may the Social Justice Movement help the disadvantaged?
>
> How may it hinder those it purports to help?

Martin Luther King Jr. addressed the topic of social justice simply by saying, "Life's most persistent and urgent question is, what are you doing for others." He believed that people should be judged "not by the color of their skin but by the content of their character."

- How does MLK's statement on Social Justice align with a Biblical understanding of how people should relate to others?
- What makes up one's character?

In his Townhall.com column *Social Justice Is No Justice at All* (March 30, 2019) psychologist, corporate speaker and author Terry Paulson wrote: "'Social justice' is a noun referring to justice in terms of the distribution of wealth, opportunities, and privileges within a society. The term is thrown around as if it is obviously a noble and good thing to work towards."

He added, "Over time, social justice has become so politically correct that to take a stand against it is anti-Christian, even anti-American. Our capitalistic system has encouraged individual achievement and has created a standard of living that is the envy of the world. It's by taking personal initiative to work hard and to earn enough to provide for yourself and your family that you can secure your own future. But somehow today, earning wealth and being rich is now a leftist sin."

While the Bible condemns greed, it does not condemn being wealthy. In fact, God himself promises to prosper those who are faithful stewards of his resources to build his kingdom. (Jeremiah 29:11)

- What is your reaction to Paulson's commentary?
- How should it be evaluated by a Christian seeking to formulate a Biblical worldview?

Some see social justice as the avenue by which a socialist utopia can be brought to a society. Their perspective is that equality of opportunity is not enough. Government must create an environment where everyone is guaranteed among other things, a minimum income, free education, and free healthcare.

> When people are dependent on the government, are they more or less likely to work towards earning and achieving their own American dream?
>
> How does government dependency affirm or devalue lives made in the image of God?

Austrian-British economist and philosopher F.A. Hayek, one of the 20th century's leading thinkers, warned, "I am certain that nothing has done so much to destroy the judicial safeguards of individual freedom as a striving after this mirage of social justice." Others who have considered the notion of social justice have called it government-legitimatized theft. Frederic Bastiat, a prominent 19th century French economist, wrote, "But how is this legal plunder to be identified? Quite simply. See if the law takes from some persons and give it to another person to whom it does not belong. See if the law benefits one citizen at the expense of another by doing what the citizen and self cannot do without committing a crime."

> How does Social Justice rob citizens of the pride of accomplishment?

Being dependent on the government may be called by some social justice but in reality it is no justice at all. It robs its citizens of the pride of the accomplishment of a life well lived, the opportunity to build a better society and the ability to accomplish the American dream.

For more than 200 years immigrants have come to America expecting a land of freedom and equal opportunity under a fair and reasonable justice system and where upward mobility allows the poor to become the middle class and some to become rich and prosperous. They come here for the hope of a better life earned through hard work and the creativity of their minds. Their goal has been and continues today to live and achieve the American dream believing everyone has the potential for success and happiness.

> ▪ How does upward economic mobility keep America "the land of opportunity?"

Finally, the thinking Christian will seek to honor God with their life and work and to find compassionate ways to keep the Great Commandment by loving their neighbor as themselves. (Luke 10:27)

> ▪ How should ideas of Social Justice inform one's Biblical worldview?

FOR FURTHER DISCUSSION OR PERSONAL REFLECTION:

How does the thinking Christian honor God with his or her life and work?

What does it mean to you to love your neighbor as yourself?

Should individuals be responsible for their success or failure?

How can the Christian church do a better job of caring for the poor?

Is a Government guaranteed minimum annual income a good idea? Why or Why not?

SESSION 11

HOW DOES YOUR WORLDVIEW ALIGN WITH BIBLICAL PRINCIPLES?

This phase of our journey to discover a Biblical worldview is complete. We have examined nine elements of a worldview to enable us to become wise and insightful thinkers. At the outset, our goal was to renew our minds with the truth of God's Word so that we will be able to think like Christians as we view and live in the culture of our society. We have reached a number of conclusions from the evidence presented in the Scriptures. Those conclusions are summarized as follows:

History—The Bible is the key to World events. A Biblical worldview of history can only be obtained by knowing the Truth of the Bible because it is His-Story, from the beginning of creation to the final judgment of mankind and eternity. God has a Master Plan for the redemption of his creation. All other utopian worldviews and "isms" start with the notion that man can save himself by good works and self sacrifice. The problem is they offer no hope for life beyond the grave by the fact that their founders are all dead. Only Jesus Christ, the foundation of the Christian worldview, is alive.

> What is it about Jesus that makes Him the foundation of the Christian Biblical worldview?

Theology

Christian theology maintains that all history, philosophy, science, mathematics, reasoning and all life experiences confirm the existence of God as the intelligent designer and creator. That he is the redeemer and the sole provider of human salvation from sin and condemnation through faith in Jesus Christ. The evidence that supports this worldview greatly exceeds the views proposed by atheism, i.e. no God.

> What has convinced you that God is the only redeemer and provider of salvation for sin? How does that renew your mind?

Philosophy

Finding answers to the profound questions of life defines one's philosophy. These questions can only be answered with a reasonable or rational Biblical philosophical worldview. True science and history support the Biblical worldview because it is the most rational. Thinking Christians believe that Jesus Christ is himself the most important philosophical truth in the Bible. The mind and wisdom of God define our reality.

> How is Jesus the most important philosophical truth?

Science

There are two controversial topics relative to a Biblical worldview of science. They come from biology and are known as Evolution and the Origins of Man. The creation speaks of a creator, God, by its beauty and symmetry and the exquisite and precise laws which govern its intelligent design. The evidence of God creating all life, including the human race, overwhelms the notion that evolution and natural forces are the explanation for human life.

> Why is Creation a more rational explanation than Evolution for the origins of man? Which worldview gives man a noble purpose?

Law

A Christian worldview of law recognizes that there are two important factors in understanding law: man's moral worth and man's rebellious or sinful nature. Because God is just and hates injustice, he has given mankind two types of law: Natural law; and Biblical law. Man has a conscience and inherently knows right from wrong which is Natural law. Biblical law centered on the 10 Commandments, comes directly from God to protect man and direct his life path because God is both loving and merciful.

> What is the interaction of the two factors that shape one's worldview of Law?

Politics and Government

The Bible advocates limited power in government. The Bible shows that all human rights are a gift of God. The Declaration of Independence states it very clearly, "We hold these truths to be self evident that all men are created equal, that they are endowed by their Creator with certain unalienable rights, that among these are life, liberty and the pursuit of happiness." Though flawed because they are comprised of sinful men and women, governments based on protecting God-given rights have proven to be more rational and just than those that prioritize the collective over the individual or allow a sovereign to dictate how men shall live.

> Why have governments based upon utopian ideologies created societies that prevent life from flourishing, crush personal liberty, and turn human happiness into misery?

Marriage and Family Life

Central to God's plan for mankind was the creation of men and women who would marry, bear and raise children, and remain faithful to one another for life. Parents would train children to follow guidelines that would help them succeed in life and foster communities that allowed individuals to grow to their potential while ensuring that the weak and infirm would be properly cared for.

> Why did God place a high value on marriage and families?

Economics

Christians know that God decreed that, "One who was not willing to work shall not eat." i.e., the Christian work ethic. With that decree came the right to own the property which produced the food. The Christian worldview is that the best economic system which will ensure checks and balances that guarantee the protection of human rights, justice under the law and personal property is Free Enterprise Capitalism. Socialism by contrast restricts marketplace and individual freedoms and gives the State control over market functions, i.e., "Big Brother."

> Which economic system would you rather live under; Socialism or Free Enterprise Capitalism? Explain your rationale.

Social Justice

The concept of social justice has become a catchphrase for the redistribution of wealth, work and compensation equality regardless of education or skills or competency. Social justice requires equality before the law not the quality of abilities, status or income. The Christian worldview is that God promises to bless those who are faithful stewards of his resources to build his kingdom therefore becoming prosperous through hard work and ingenuity in itself is not a sin. Thinking Christians will honor God with their lives and work and find compassionate ways to keep the Great Commandment, to love their neighbor as themselves.

> What does the Great Commandment have to do with holding a Christian worldview of society, equality and justice?

FOR FURTHER DISCUSSION OR PERSONAL REFLECTION:

As our journey draws to a close, what other questions or topics would you like to ask or explore as you acquire or reinforce a Biblical worldview?

How has this study challenged you to Renew your Mind and embrace God's Wisdom?

How has this study enabled you to understand your Christian worldview and prepare you to defend it?

Do you believe that you are now better able to contend for and defend your Christian faith, to Think as a Christian? What are the next steps you should take to build your confidence?

(Note: Discussion Leader to Review the Gems of Wisdom in the Appendix)

EPILOGUE

During the 11 sessions of this study, you've sampled a bit of what we identify as a Christian worldview. By no means comprehensive, this study was intended to get you talking with others about the challenges faced by Christians throughout history and the ones facing them today. Questions have guided your time of dialog during this study. We'd like to leave you with a few more to consider on your own.

1. Are you willing to ask Jesus to give you a new beginning with him and transform your life?

2. Can you make following him your highest priority?

3. What would you tell someone else about what you're learning about Jesus and what it means to have a Christian worldview?

4. Are you willing to share the Good News about him with others in your world?

As you continue to journey with Jesus, please remember that you are not traveling alone. He's gone ahead of you to blaze the trail, and he promises to be with you every step of the way. He promises to give a purposeful, flourishing and meaningful life now and for eternity to all who journey with him, to each person who affirms that Jesus is Lord and Savior. Moreover, he has promised to provide the wisdom, the power and even the words you need to invite others to follow him, too.

If you enjoyed this study of Christian worldview, you may want to study the life of Jesus as told by the Apostle Mark. *YOUR INVITATION* is an 11-session small-group exploration designed to deepen your understanding of God's love and forgiveness as expressed in the life and teachings of Jesus Christ.

The principal doctrines of Christianity as laid down by the Apostle Paul in his letter to the church in Rome make a fascinating study. *LIGHTING THE WAY* is a 12-session small-group exploration of those teachings and doctrines that have guided the Church for two millennia.

You may also want to consider studying the life of Jesus as told by the Apostle John. *TRANSFORMATION* is a 13-session small-group exploration designed to deepen your understanding of God's love and forgiveness as expressed in the life and teachings of Jesus Christ.

YOUR INVITATION, *LIGHTING THE WAY*, and *TRANSFORMATION* from Living Dialog Ministries, are available at **LivingDialog.org** and from online retailers and bookstores everywhere.

Please visit our sister website, **LifesBasicQuestions.com**, for a place to engage some of the core questions of life. The website is designed to be a user-friendly way to dialog about the kinds of issues you encountered in your study of Paul's letter to the Romans. There is also a place on the website for visitors to ask their own questions, and receive a confidential response from the Living Dialog Ministry team. It's a helpful, no-cost resource you can share with others.

APPENDIX

- Apologetics — What is It?
- Man's Noble Purpose
- Love God with all Your Mind
- Conscience — Mind's Partner
- Why different Versions of the Bible
- What is Repentance?
- The Law of Non-Contradiction
- Why Memorize Bible Verses
- What does God want for His children?
- Apostles Creed — Nicene Creed
- Christianity vs. Other Religions
- Economics — Macro and Micro
- My Friend *by D. J. Higgins*

Apologetics — What is it?

This question and topic generally today refers to Christianity. The word apologetics is somewhat misleading and has nothing to do with apologizing in the modern sense of the word. Apologetics is building the case for explaining and defending the Christian faith. So, the straightforward answer is that apologetics defines, "What Christians Believe and Why Christians Believe It."

First, an examination of the 'What is Believed' includes knowledge about God, creation, nature, origins of man, sin, morality, stewardship, life's purpose, Jesus Christ, redemption, salvation, Heaven, Hell, the Christian church, the Bible, the Old Testament history of nations, End Times and eternity, for starters.

Then there is the second part of apologetics, 'Why Christians Believe It'. Christians start with a concept that the Bible is the inspired word of God and therefore totally reliable as truth about what it contains. They trust the evidence that proves the Bible is historically correct, that it is the best documented of all ancient books and that it contains prophecy that is 100% accurate as only God could see the future of human history as if it is already completed. The Bible is a miracle in its own right as it was written over a period of 1600 years by 40 authors in complete harmony and without any contradictions.

Christians trust and believe the evidence of both Biblical and secular records, (Josephus AD 75 & Tacitus AD 116), of the life, teaching, miracles, death by crucifixion, resurrection (witnessed by over 500 people) and ascension to heaven of Jesus Christ. They further believe the evidence of the dramatically transformed lives of Jesus' 12 disciples who boldly proclaimed the truth of the gospel and were martyred for their testimonies.

Then there is the miraculous contribution of Christianity to Western Civilization; literature, art, science, music, mathematics, medicine, education, philosophy, law and much more.

Finally, there is the witness and testimonies of the hundreds of millions of followers of Jesus Christ through the centuries. Why so many believers? The answer is because Jesus is the only way to eternal life and a transformed life full of meaning and purpose. He is 'The Way' to receive God's gifts of joy, love, peace, forgiveness, contentment, faith and eternal hope.

Man's Noble Purpose

Man has a noble purpose. A purpose that is good and honorable. A purpose that can be admired due to its impressive value in the work and activity of God.

What is man that God is mindful of Him? (Ps. 8:4). God created man, a little lower than the angels (Ps. 8:5), with a purpose to rule over the planet Earth (Gen. 1:28). This purpose was in direct conflict with the former most powerful ruler of Earth, Satan. Satan attacks man to remove man as ruler and for Satan to take back his rulership of Earth.

But, Jesus the Lord God takes on flesh of a man (Heb. 2:9), coming to Earth as the "son of man." This son of man defeats Satan, and is crowned with glory and honor (Heb. 2:9; Ps. 8:5). Jesus raises man to a highly elevated position as a son of God and brother of Jesus, through placement in Christ (Eph. 2:6) and adoption as sons (Gal. 4:4-5), for those who receive him (Jn. 1:12). Man is thus raised to the highest place of significance far above that of the powerful Satan.

Such a work of God brings glory to God revealing his wonderful grace and mercy.

Further, after having raised man to a high position in Christ, God then uses man to join with Him in order to carry out God's will on Earth. This working occurs (1) through man's relationship with God, in that man by prayer asks God to carry out God's will on planet Earth (1Jn. 5:14-15; Rom. 12:2) and (2) by God working in and through man as man presents himself a living sacrifice, holy and acceptable to God (Col. 1:13; Rom. 12:1). God's will is to make sons of God from man and to disciple such sons, resulting in man bringing glory to God by praise, honor, thanksgiving, worship, service, obedience, and devotion to Him (1Pet. 2:9; Ps. 100:2-4).

Man's purpose is thus: To be an instrument used by God in the face of a powerful enemy, wherein God rules planet Earth through man, to accomplish God's purposes, and so bring glory to God (1Pet. 4:11; Eph. 1:12; 1Cor 10:31).

Love the Lord your God with all your Mind?

This challenge for all Christians comes directly from the great Commandment recorded in Luke 10:27. It is a confirmation Jesus made about the importance of using intellect and reason needed to become a mature follower and disciple. So, how does a Christian do it; i.e. "Love God with all your mind."

Jesus provided the way to love God with your mind by giving all new believers the indwelling of the Holy Spirit to lead them to life-transforming truths found throughout the Bible. What is required on the believer's part is to be diligent in using his or her God-given faculties to gain relevant knowledge and understanding by reading, studying, examining and discussing Biblical truths.

This pursuit of truth will also lead to grasping the meaning of Apologetics, i.e. What Christians believe and why they believe it. This intellectual undertaking, guided by the Holy Spirit, will also over time result in being able to discern truth from cultural lies and justify one's beliefs about all things important. Those faculties we are given to use include common sense and sense of curiosity, memory, logical reasoning abilities and our moral conscience.

Scientists have demonstrated that reason and logical thinking differentiate man from all other creatures. These capabilities also confirm that mankind was created in the image of God. These unique qualities imply the importance of using our mind and intellect to enter into an intimate and personal relationship with God and with Jesus Christ. Eventually the believer will be capable of thinking like a Christian in all elements or disciplines encountered in life and in the culture and will have developed a Biblical worldview.

For a more in-depth study of this topic, we recommend the book by J. P. Moreland, *Love Your God with All Your Mind* and *Your Mind Matters* by John Stott. An important follow-up question which will be answered in the future is, Where is your mind and why is that important? You might be surprised at the answer.

Conscience — Your Mind's Partner

Your conscience is an essential component of being created in God's image. The conscience is present in every human being from birth. It is the soul's warning system, which allows human beings to contemplate their motives and actions and make moral decisions/evaluations of what is right and what is wrong. It allows and it enables a person to discern between good and evil, fact and fiction, truth and opinion and what is real and what is not.

The conscience is a companion of the mind and the heart in the soul of every person. The conscience must be informed to the highest moral and spiritual standard, which only happens when it is submitted to the control of the Holy Spirit through knowing God's Word. The conscience plays an important roll in developing a Biblical worldview. God's Holy Spirit is the agent that opens the conscience to truth.

(Source- John McArthur Bible Commentary, Page 1617)

Why Different Versions of The Bible?

There was a time when the Christian church had only one Version of the Bible. During the Middle Ages, the Bible as we know it today, had been translated from the original sources into Latin. It was put into the hands of the Church clergy who were charged with teaching it to the people. The Bible is God's living Word, our guide to faith and practice.

The church experienced a great transformation in the 15th and 16th centuries. The Bible was freed from the control of the clergy and put it into the hands and hearts of the people. It was translated into the language of common usage. The invention of the printing press greatly enhanced the ability to make Bibles available on a global basis. Today, translators regularly view ancient Scriptures and write down how they believe the words of Greek and Hebrew can best be restated in modern English. A great deal of tedious study of multiple manuscripts goes into every chapter and verse as scholars debate which words and phrases will best convey the intent and meaning of the original.

The message of the Bible is always the same, the unfolding drama of redemption and salvation. It is the old, old story of Jesus and his love. It is the gospel, the good news of forgiveness and new life in Christ. (Romans 10:9&10)

The Bible is not meant to be an object to be admired and worshiped but to be God's invitation to come to a personal relationship with our Heavenly Father and gain the assurance of eternal life and Heaven. The Bible is a story to be told! It is the greatest story ever written. One that is supremely worth telling over and over again. Yes, the Bible comes to us in many different versions but the story is the same. Do you know it? Love will find a way to get it told. Are you willing to tell the story. There are still many who have not heard the Good news.

What is Repentance?

Repentance is being sorry for doing wrong. True repentance requires changing behavior. Many understand the term repentance to mean "turning from sin." This is not the Biblical definition of repentance. In the Bible, the word repent means "to change one's mind." The Bible also tells us that true repentance will result in a change of actions. (Acts 3:19)

The apostle Paul declares, "I preached that they should repent and turn to God to prove their repentance by deeds." (Acts 26:20) The Biblical definition of repentance is a change of mind that results in a change of action. Repentance and faith are actually like two sides of a coin . . . we turn from our old sinful ways and turn to the Lord for salvation and newness of life.

Repentance is the desire to turn away from sin and restore one's relationship with God. Repentance is a decision of the mind and the heart with genuine sorrow over sin. It is an initial step when a person decides to put his or her faith in Jesus Christ as Lord and Savior. It is not necessarily a one time event. In fact, it is an ongoing process after a person has been saved or born again and becomes a new creation in Christ. (Romans 10:9&10)

One needs to repent in order to keep an open personal relationship with Jesus and experience peace with God. Repentance clears away any barriers that can inhibit a truthful dialog and an intimate personal prayerful conversation with God. All prayers are to be offered in Jesus name because He is the only advocate and intercessor with God.

A person who has fully repented and decided to follow Jesus Christ will give evidence of a changed life. (2 Corinthians 5:17; Galatians 5:19-23) Repentance properly defined and lived out is evidence of being a "New Creation" in Christ. Biblical repentance is changing your mind about your need for Jesus Christ as Savior and turning to God in faith to receive salvation and eternal life. Turning from sin is not the definition of repentance, but is one of the results of genuine, faith-based repentance towards the Lord Jesus Christ. In 1 John 1:9 we read; "If we confess our sins, Jesus is faithful to forgive us our sins and purify us from all unrighteousness." It is the way we clean our hearts and our minds. It is Repentance!

The Law of Non-Contradiction

In the process of 'Renewing your Mind' and learning to 'Think like a Christian', it is important, in fact critical, to be able to identify objective truth in the various elements of the culture on a journey to acquire a Christian or Biblical worldview. Truth exists and can be discovered through a process that thoroughly examines the evidence that is consistent with reality. The Bible is the source of God's truth and a thorough examination of its contents is the only way to renew your mind and develop an accurate lens through which to view the world we live in.

Michael Edwards book, *Gravity*, provides a definition of the law of non-contradiction. He describes it as, "our built-in lie detector to help us find truth." This law is commonly understood in that opposite ideas cannot both be true at the same time. The most frequently cited example, which is easily understood, is that the earth cannot be both flat and round at the same time. Edward states, "That knowledge of this law is crucial to understanding that truth does exist and it's opposite is always false.

In our culture today many people believe that they can have their own truth. You can often hear statements like, "that may be true for you but it's not for me." In the discipline of science, it is important to follow the evidence and see where it leads before the scientist reaches a conclusion. The same principle applies when searching the Scriptures to discover God's Truth about creation or the origins of man, philosophy, the law both natural and Biblical, and even disciplines like economics, politics, social justice, morality and property rights. Diligent search of the objective evidence in the Scriptures will lead to the discovery of objective truth, God's truth.

Feelings, opinions and beliefs are important but they are not necessarily true no matter how sincere. On this journey, the law of non-contradiction must be applied to experience a renewing of your mind and gaining a Biblical worldview. Truth Matters!

Why Memorize Bible Verses

God has promised a number of benefits that can be ours as a result of storing His Word in our mind and our hearts. The Bible has thousands of promises God wants us to know and claim for our own. Listed below are some of the benefits:

Victory over Sin

"How can a young man keep his way pure? By living according to your word. I have hidden your word in my heart that I might not sin against you."

Psalm 119:9-11

Spiritual Growth

"But his delight is in the law of the Lord, and on his law he meditates day and night. He is like a tree planted by streams of water, which uses fruit in season and whose leaf does not wither. Whatever he does prospers."

Psalm 1:2-3

Renewing Your Mind

"... Be transformed by the renewing of your mind. Then you will be able to test and approve what God's will is—His good, pleasing and perfect will."

Romans 12:1-2

Inner Joy

"When your words came; ... they were my joy and my heart's delight."

Jerermiah 15:16

Answers to Prayer

"if you remain in me and my words remain in you, ask whatever you wish and it will be given to you."

John 15:16

Wisdom and Understanding

"The fear of the Lord is the beginning of wisdom and the knowledge of the Holy One is understanding." "Oh how I love your law! . . . Your commands make me wiser than my enemies, for they are ever with me . . . I have more understanding than the elders, for I obey your precepts."

Proverbs 9:10, Psalm 119:97-100

Defeat Satan's Schemes

"Finally, be strong in the Lord and in his mighty power. Put on the full armor of God so that you can take your stand against the devil's schemes . . . Take the helmet of salvation and the sword of the spirit, which is the word of God."

Ephesians 6:10-11,17

Shell Point Academy of Lifelong Learning — May 3, 2021
Copyright 2021, Medina Ministries

What does God want for His Children?

TRUST: In Him as Creator and Father of the Lord Jesus Christ. (Genesis 1:1)

BELIEVE : In Jesus as Lord and Savior. (John 1:1-5, 1John 5:12)

LOVE : God and your neighbor as yourself. (Luke 10:27)

TRUTH : Know God's living Word, The Bible, and live it!

MEMORIZE IT. (John 14:6, John 8:32)

SHARE : The Gospel — The Great Commission, as you are going in life each day. (Matthew 28:19)

OBEY : His Commandments "10" (Exodus 20)

GRACE : Receive His Salvation and blessings with Gratitude. (Ephesians 2:8)

MERCY : Be Thankful for His Protection & Forgiveness — His mercies are new and fresh every morning.

PURIFICATION : Be made Righteous & Holy (1 John 1:9)

SANCTIFICATION : Become more like Jesus every day in every way (Predestined) (Ephesians 1:4-6)

QUIET TIME : Set aside a time for a daily experience with Him to know God more fully and intimately. A time of prayer and reflection and to discern God's will; His good, pleasing and perfect will for your life. (Romans 12:2) A time to let go let and let God rule and reign in your life. A time to enjoy just being in God's presence, to experience fully His unfailing love, to be immersed in His Amazing Grace, to reflect on His Promises, to be renewed by the Holy Spirit, to receive His 'marching orders' for the day and to commit to live life so as to Honor Him in everything.

WORSHIP : Be an Active member in a local Christ-centered, Bible-preaching church. Attend services each week, including a Sunday school class. Be a faithful steward of your time, talents and treasures. Participate in the Fellowship of believers in Jesus Christ. Make time for a Bible study and join a "Small Group."

The Apostles Creed

I believe in God the Father Almighty, Maker of heaven and earth. And in Jesus Christ, His only Son, our Lord; Who was conceived by the Holy Spirit; Born of the Virgin Mary; Suffered under Pontius Pilate; Was crucified, dead and buried; He descended into Hell; The third day He rose again from the dead; He ascended into heaven; And sitteth on the right hand of God the Father

Almighty; From thence He shall come to judge the living and the dead. I believe in the Holy Spirit; The Holy Christian Church, the Communion of Saints; The Forgiveness of sins; The Resurrection of the body; And the life everlasting. Amen.

The Nicene Creed

I believe in one God, the Father almighty, maker of heaven and earth and of all things visible and invisible. And in one Lord Jesus Christ, the only-begotten Son of God, begotten of the Father before all ages, God of God, Light of Light, very God of very God, begotten not made, being of one substance with the Father, through Whom all things were made: Who for us men and for our salvation came down from heaven, was incarnate by the Holy Spirit of the virgin Mary, and was made man: Who for us, too, was crucified under Pontius Pilate, suffered, and was buried: the third day He rose according to the Scriptures, ascended into heaven, and is seated on the right hand of the Father: He shall come again with glory to judge the living and the dead, and His kingdom shall have no end. And in the Holy Spirit, the Lord and Giver of life, Who proceeds from the Father and the Son: Who together with the Father and the Son is worshiped and glorified: Who spoke by the prophets. And I believe one holy, Christian, and apostolic Church. I acknowledge one baptism for the remission of sins, and I look for the resurrection of the dead and life of the age to come. Amen.

Christianity vs. Other World Religions

Listed below are several brief perspectives from several Bible scholars and pastors on the primary difference between Christianity and all other world religions. As a composite, they offer a robust presentation of the superiority of Christianity as the one and only faith that promises assurance of forgiveness of sins, peace with God and eternal life. Jesus resurrection is the foundation upon which the Christian faith is based.

The simple answer is, Jesus! Why? Because He alone saves. (Jn. 14:6)

Only Christianity offers absolute assurance of eternal life as it is a gift of God's grace for all who by faith trust in Jesus as Savior and Lord. (Ephesians 2:8).Christianity is about Jesus, the Cross (forgiveness of sins) and his Resurrection and Ascension and his second coming.

The founders of all other religions are dead. They have offered some sound platitudes for living a moral life, but no hope for eternity based on solid evidence. They are religions of good works and self-sacrifice to gain a pardon for the worshiper's sins.

The person of Jesus Christ and the Holy Bible differentiate Christianity. The cross of Christ forever bridged the gap between sinners and a Holy God. The Bible, rightly called the book that made our world, has inspired the best of Western civilization: science, technology, education, and political and economic freedom. Because we are made in God's image, Christianity values human dignity and liberates those who are often marginalized in other cultures: slaves, women, children and outcasts.

Christianity's primary doctrine is that all of the worshipper's sins/wrongdoings, including those past, present and future have been paid for by God himself and such a pardon as a gift from God accepted once by faith in His Son Jesus who paid the penalty for such sins by his death on the cross. Whereas, all other religions require good works and religious activity of the worshippers to gain a pardon for the worshipers sins.

Christianity is unique in that it experiences and believes there is inside the Godhead an all embracing, self-giving, dynamic love between Father, Son and Holy Spirit, so it can be truly said, "God is Love."

Mankind feels the need for a power beyond itself but often defines that from man's finitude. Mankind makes images, fashions theologies to negotiate and "cut" deals with God developing rituals which often misrepresent God. Christianity represents God as all powerful, all knowing, present everywhere, whose Nature is Love, who redeems and empowers those who accept and trust God's Grace. (i.e. salvation in Jesus Christ)

Christian Faith, is not man made, but God revealed! Therefore of universal validity, based on the conviction of the deity, authority and exclusive claims of the historic Christ as revealed in the Bible. Christ was (and is) Himself the message. The answer to the fundamental question of all religion, "Can I know God? What is He like?" has been given in the life, death and resurrection of the Lord Jesus Christ, for the barrier of sin which separates man from God is removed. It is just here, that Christianity is unique! Other religions teach what man must do, Christianity alone tells what God has already done in Christ.

Two phrases differentiate Christianity from all other world religions;

"in order that" and "because of." 'In order that' you can gain favor with God, you must keep ALL the rituals and make ALL the sacrifices. The reality is that in other religions you never know if or when you have done enough. Where as, with Christianity, 'because of' Jesus Christ (Ephesians 2:8) you can have a relationship and peace with God, have you sins forgiven, receive the gift of eternal life and have the absolute certainty of Heaven. (Jn. 14:6 & 1 John 5:12) World religions are man made. Christianity is God Inspired.

In Christianity salvation is, by God's Grace alone, by Faith alone, in Christ alone! Only Jesus saves! (Ephesians 2:8) Forgiveness of sins, Peace with God and eternal life are found in no other religion.

Economics: Macro and Micro Basics

ECONOMICS: The branch of knowledge concerned with the production, consumption and transfer of wealth; a measure of the material prosperity and productivity of a region or nation.

There are basically three main factors that define economics, they are; output/productivity (GDP), employment rates and monetary policy (inflation) considerations. Output is best defined as the sum of all value added (goods & services) in the economy.

MACRO ECONOMICS: decision-making within and economy as a whole from local and regional to global.

The primary indicators are GDP, unemployment rates, per capita income, price indices/ inflation/ deflation, International trade balances (deficit versus surplus), International finance and currency evaluations,

MICRO ECONOMICS: decision-making and behavior of individuals and firms in making choices in narrowly defined markets of local goods and services.

NOTE: unemployment generally occurs when growth stagnates, i.e. below 2.5-3.0% and when there are significant structural shifts to new industries and new technologies.

My Friend

by, D. J. Higgins

My friend I stand in judgment now
And I feel that you are to blame somehow
In earth I walked with you day by day
And never did you point the way.

You knew the Lord and in truth and glory
And never did you tell the story.
My knowledge then was very dim
You could have let me say to Him.

Though we lived together here on earth,
You never told me of the second birth.
And now I stand this day condemned
Because you failed to mention Him.

You taught me many things, that's true,
I called you friend and trusted you.
But I learned now that it's too late
You could have saved me from this fate.

We walked by me and talked by night
And yet you showed me not the light
You let me live, love and die
You knew I'd never live on high.

Yes, I called you friend in life
And trusted you through joy and strife
And yet on coming to the end,
I cannot, now call you friend!

ACKNOWLEDGEMENTS

I owe a deep sense of gratitude and many thanks to the men's Discovery Dialogue Group of Sanibel Community Church for the many challenging sessions we spent over the past two years searching for and discovering what it means to think and reason like a Christian and to develop and live with a Biblical Worldview of the culture of the society in which we live. In these many dialogue sessions we gained new insights, greater clarity and deeper understanding of what it means to think like a Christian. Our process was to inquire not advocate, explore but not argue and to discover not to convince. As a result of these engaging sessions, we were able to reach consensus on the Biblical perspectives of our culture as presented in this study. When a person completes this 10 week study, we believe it will enable each participant to renew their minds with the truth of the Scriptures and reason and think more clearly as a follower of Jesus Christ.

More specifically I would like to thank Pierre Loizeaux for his presentation on Biblical History, pastors Rev. Hu Auburn, Rev. Chris Scruggs and Rev. Irving Stubbs for their insights and comments on Theology, Lee Southard for his insightful text on Biology and the Origins of Man, Jim Kelly for his contribution to the topic of philosophy, to Allen Hye for his enlightening text on Politics and

Government, Larry Jarvis for his thoughts and contributions on the topic of Law, both Natural and Biblical, and Russ Warren, Dave Dannemiller and Pete Dannemiller for their review and comments and constructive edits on the subject of Economics.

I am also indebted to Brian Regrut, Executive Director of Living Dialog Ministries for his thorough edit of the entire text and for his insightful comments to make it better and for session 7 on Marriage and Family. Further, I want to thank the Board of Living Dialog Ministries including Harry Pollard, Irving Stubbs and Ken Engelke for their support and encouragement on this study. This will be the fourth study in our Living Dialog series which includes the titles, *YOUR INVITATION*, *TRANSFORMATION* and *LIGHTING THE WAY*. This study would never have been conceived if it weren't for the excellent textbook, *Thinking Like A Christian*, created by David Noebel and published by Summit Ministries. His work got us thinking about our own Biblical worldview and the idea of renewing one's mind. Those revelations are what inspired the writing of this study.

Another special thanks to the design concepts of Frank Gutbrod who created the eye-catching front cover and chapter header designs for the interior pages. Frank was the creative resource also for the covers of our prior three studies in the Living Dialog series.

Finally, and most importantly, thanks to my Lord and Savior Jesus Christ and the Holy Spirit who inspired the writing of the study. They were along beside me these past two years as we labored together in creating this publication. I also received great encouragement and inspiration from my beloved wife Jean Marie who was with me when we started this project but is now home in Heaven with our Lord Jesus. I know she will be pleased that this work of love is finally complete and published.

ABOUT US
Directors of the Living Dialog Ministries

JOHN C. [JACK] DANNEMILLER, Chairman and CEO of *The Living Dialog Ministries*, is the former Chair and CEO of Applied Industrial Technologies, a Fortune 1000 corporation. He is a 30-year leader of small group Bible studies, a frequent speaker at Christian Businessmen events, and a lecturer at the Weatherhead Graduate School of Business of Case Western Reserve University where he was honored with the Distinguished Alumni Award.

IRVING R. STUBBS, President Emeritous of *The Living Dialog Ministries*, is a minister with degrees from Davidson College and Union Theological Seminary in New York. He served in pastorates, an urban ministry, and consultant to business, media, religious, government, and professional organizations and their executives in North America, Europe, and Asia. He is the author and co-author of books, articles, and learning resources.

HENRY R. [HARRY] POLLARD, IV, Secretary of *The Living Dialog Ministries*, is Chairman, Partner, and Practicing Attorney with Parker, Pollard, Wilton & Peaden, PC of Richmond, Virginia where he has practiced law for more than 40 years. He has served as an officer and director of numerous businesses including banking, real estate, and financial entities. He is co-founder and Chairman of The Values Institute of America.

KENT E. ENGELKE, Treasurer of *The Living Dialog Ministries*, is a Managing Director and Chief Economic Strategist for Capitol Securities Management, a $6.1 billion asset management company, and has served as a director of several publicly traded banks and mortgage banking firms. His views on the economy and the markets are routinely solicited by major media outlets. He credits God for the words he writes daily and thanks God for courage and perseverance in overcoming obstacles.

BRIAN N. REGRUT, Executive Director of *The Living Dialog Ministries*, is a former public relations executive and consultant, corporate speech writer, author and lecturer serving clients in the fields of telecommunications, financial services and education. He has served in a variety of church leadership roles including preaching and teaching. He and his wife of more than 50 years have taught Sunday School together and have led small group Bible studies for many years.

A THOUGHT-PROVOKING EVANGELISM TOOL FOR CHURCHES AND ORGANIZATIONS

For those on a journey of discovery, finally answers to the profound questions of life. This little book has been distributed to thousands.

Available in bulk at a reasonable cost with a customized cover featuring your logo and message from your church or organization.

Join the dialog
www.lifesbasicquestions.com

For pricing email
info@LivingDialog.org

WOULD YOU LIKE TO HAVE A CONVERSATION WITH JESUS?

Our Study Guides for small groups will allow you to become immersed in the truth of God's word, answering questions as if you were having a conversation with Jesus or Paul the Apostle.

YOUR INVITATION

Each of the 11 sessions starts with a thought-provoking question that leads the group into a short, biblically-accurate narrative interspersed with questions the group can use as dialog starters.

LIGHTING THE WAY

This 12-session guide leads groups through an exploration of the Paul's letter to followers of Christ who lived in Rome. Here you'll engage in dialog about the principal doctrines of Christianity.

TRANSFORMATION

is designed to lead your small group through a rewarding study of the life Jesus as related by the Apostle John. During the 13 sessions you will engage with others in an interactive format allowing you to gain new insights into Jesus, God's son and mankind's savior.

Order your Study Guides today at LivingDialog.org
or from your favorite bookseller.

ANSWERS TO YOUR GREATEST QUESTIONS
A Journey in Discovering God's Wisdom

The genius of this book is that it takes a Biblical Christian Worldview in answering many profound and soul-searching questions about life and faith. It is a must-read for any person seeking God's truth for living a meaningful, purposeful and joyful life now and for eternity.

Order from
www.LivingDialog.org
or your favorite bookseller.

www.ingramcontent.com/pod-product-compliance
Lightning Source LLC
Chambersburg PA
CBHW072052290426
44110CB00014B/1646